Praise for
Smart Marketing Execution

"I thought when I picked up this book, *"Oh God, not another marketing book ... <sigh>"* I hate fluff. This is not fluff. What is valuable to me: A clear road map, why I should follow it and what I get if I do it right. That's what Clare has written. Marketing for people who are operationally focused on getting things done. If you are one of those people, get this book and a pen, you'll be writing a lot of notes."

Tom Searcy, Author of *Whale Hunting* and *How To Close A Deal Like Warren Buffett*

"You hold in your hands a philosophy and approach to marketing in a new world of opportunity. Keep Clare's book within arms' reach and refer to it often. She shines a bright light on how to sell your products and services and accelerate your results. You will find her insights and ideas practical, proven-to-work and immediately accessible. Count me a fan!"

Mark LeBlanc, CSP, author of *Never Be The Same* and *Growing Your Business!*

"Ideas are great, but the money is in execution! *Smart Marketing Execution* is a no-fluff roadmap to growth, period."

John Jantsch, author of *Duct Tape Marketing* and *The Ultimate Marketing Engine*

"This book provides an outline of how to strategize smarter combined with great anecdotes and tools to put Clare's marketing knowledge into action. A must read!"

Lisa Apolinski, CMC, author of *Grow Your Market Share In A Zombie Apocalypse*

"Too many marketing leaders fly by the seat of their pants. Their annual marketing strategy and planning can amount to, "Here are our goals and here's how we might achieve those goals, but let's assess and adapt along the way."

I should know. I've been guilty of this line of thinking more than once. For a better way, *Smart Marketing Execution* by Clare F. Price is a must read. Clare's framework, what she calls the "integrated marketing operating system," will help you and your marketing teams deliver profitability, productivity and operating efficiency."

Dennis Shiao, CEO, Attention Retention

"*Smart Marketing Execution* lives up to its name. It brings clarity and focus to a big, complicated subject. The tools in the book provide an easy-to-use approach that hones in on the right place for your business to start. It has helped me to understand how to identify the right tribe to sell to for my business, saving time, money and a whole lot of frustration for me and my team."

Rosemary Paetow, author of *Better Bigger Bolder*, with Bob Sher

"I recently had the opportunity to read and fully digest Clare Price's book, *Smart Marketing Execution*. I am going to begin this evaluation by revealing that I have read a lot of business books from experts that advise their customers on how to run their businesses, develop their products, market their products, target the correct clientele, and more. *Smart Marketing Execution* is unique in that Clare gives all of the details on 'how to' rather than simply what and why. In addition to providing what and why, Clare provides a comprehensive MBA-like learning experience. You can learn a lot as you work your way through the book, but what's truly important is that the tools, techniques and plans are right in front of you. Clare guides business owners and leaders through the exact things they need to do to become more effective leaders, but she also gives them a better understanding of their business and markets. At the end, you'll see that the payoff is worth it."

Steve Pappas, host of the Science of CX Podcast

SMART MARKETING EXECUTION

How To Accelerate Profitability, Performance, And Productivity

CLARE F. PRICE

Printed in the United States of America.

ISBN-13: 978-1-957651-17-0
Library of Congress Control Number: 2022914865

Designed by

INDIE BOOKS INTERNATIONAL, INC.
2511 WOODLANDS WAY
OCEANSIDE, CA 92054
www.indiebooksintl.com

DEDICATION

To my cousin, Elizabeth White Caputo, for her unfailing love and support of all my crazy ideas.

Denise,

To your success!

Enjoy!

[illegible]

TABLE OF CONTENTS

PREFACE

How do you turn a one-million-dollar company into a ten million dollar one? Smart execution. A ten-million-dollar company into a hundred-million-dollar company? Smart execution. A hundred-million-dollar company into a billion-dollar company? Smart execution. Smart execution enables a corporation to achieve its vision, plans, and goals. Smart execution separates the economic winners from the losers.

Here's a cautionary tale.

Dennis Bradley, director of network systems for a Silicon Valley tech giant, was a firefighter. He was proud of it. Proud of the way his team always came through when they had flames licking at their heels. Trouble was most of Bradley's fires were of his own making.

The big event each year for Bradley's group was Dreamforce, the major Salesforce convention held annually in San Francisco. Every year, Bradley, in full firefighter mode, geared up for the event about eight weeks out. He got his team of programmers, designers, marketers, salespersons, and booth builders together; barked out their marching orders; and got everyone scrambling at a fever pitch. Nights, weekends, all-nighters, and missed vacations and family time. Thousands of dollars in rush charges for overtime. It didn't matter! They had to make it happen. And they did. No one was more pleased than Bradley. At the post-show meeting, he chanted his familiar refrain: "We were in the weeds, people, but we pulled it out and got it done. Great job everyone."

In his enthusiasm for a job well done, he didn't always notice the brain drain as top talent left his team every year for another role in the organization or with a competitor. Nor did he notice the fact that his cost overruns meant his group could not attend one or more of the smaller shows during the rest of the year.

By contrast, Akim Camaron, director of software services, used his post-Dreamforce meeting to debrief his team and start planning for the next year. They used takeaways from the last show to lay the foundation for the future. They developed a road map with monthly project milestones eleven months in advance. They finalized the structure for the event, booth details, and theme. Camaron worked months in advance with product development to showcase new products. His team had time to assess the competition to better position the company and its products to attendees. They had flexibility to make changes. His team collaborated, worked smoothly, and had the energy and enthusiasm during the show to have fun with each other and trade show prospects. His team got the job done using smart marketing execution.

Here are two questions: Which team would you rather lead? Which team would you rather be on?

This book was written as antidote to the number one business killer of all time: poor execution of business and marketing strategy. The solution is to replace trial-and-error, "pray and spray" marketing with an integrated marketing operating system that delivers profitability, productivity, and operating efficiency.

That system, the Octain Growth System (OGS), integrates strategy, execution, and automation to provide business builders and marketers with a proven pathway to profitability. To ensure your success, OGS provides you with an experienced Growth Architect. Our GAs are certified OGS consultants with the tools, training, and talent to support vision and business growth goals.

PART I:

GROWTH DEMYSTIFIED

Chapter 1
EXPLODING THE GROWTH MYTH

PERHAPS THESE BUSINESS clichés sound familiar:

"Let's throw it against the wall and see if it sticks."
"Let's run it up the flagpole and see who salutes."
"We like to fly by the seat of our pants."
"Assess and pivot. It's the only way to go."

They all reflect the use of trial-and-error decision-making, a practice so common, so accepted, and so widely used that business builders naturally gravitate to it. This approach is so ingrained in our corporate DNA that most of us wouldn't know how to run our businesses without it.

I know I never did. Until I learned that this pervasive business practice is one of the costliest and most time-consuming business crushers of all time.

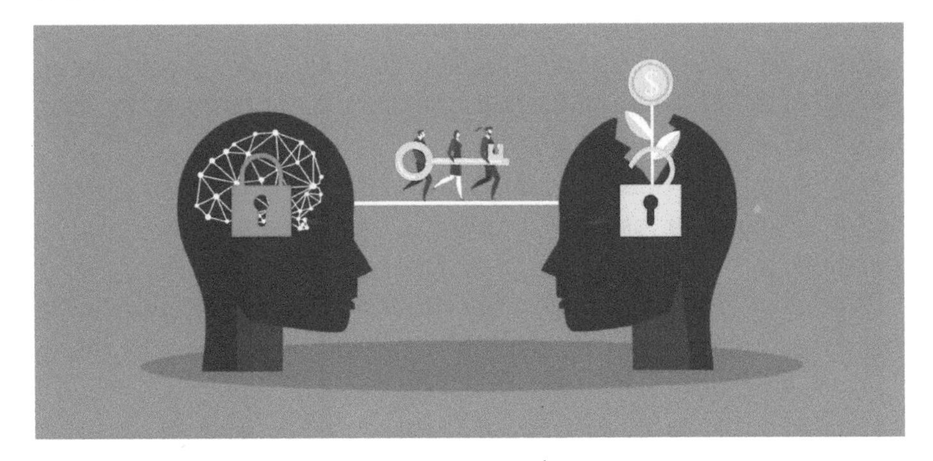

It was January 2000. The world was poised on the bright beginning of a new year and a new decade. It was the start of the new millennium. I was working as the VP of marketing at a software start-up in Mountain View, California, building a new analytics platform for measuring customer experience. We had an innovative product solution, a dedicated technical team, and a brash, young, visionary CEO with a lot to prove to his father, one of the Silicon Valley's most notable serial entrepreneurs.

Despite everything we had going for us, we started the new year in a panic. We were almost out of cash. The consumer analytics market was so new that our engineers had to innovate and create their own road map. Of course, they ran into glitch after glitch on their way to success, rapidly burning through our seed funding. If we didn't get a new round of funding soon, we would have to shut the doors.

We had a good track record at our stage and an easy story to tell: *You can't change what you can't measure.* As the new century dawned, customers' expectations were changing faster than ever. We had *the solution.*

The CEO and I met with just about every investor in town and his reaction to those meetings shone the light of truth on the true cost of trial-and-error decision-making. Every time we met with a new investor, they had ideas about what we could do with the product and our marketing story. They weren't investing, just giving feedback.

However, that didn't matter to my CEO. He'd go rushing back to the technical team and demand all the changes the investor had suggested, burning up more time and capital, sowing more chaos with every new meeting. We never got that next round of funding. Before the sun set on the first year of the new millennium, we were out of business. In addition, I learned a very valuable lesson.

Just about everything we believe about the value of trial-and-error decision-making, or "assess and pivot," as it is now commonly called, is a myth.

When you throw it up against the wall and see if it sticks, you mostly end up with dirty walls. It's easy to assess and pivot your way into a financial quagmire. Sustainable growth it's not.

Five Big Growth Killers

Trial-and-error decision-making is one of the biggest growth myths out there. But it's not the only one. Do any of these sound familiar?

Hamster-Wheel Marketing. Hamster-wheel marketing feels exactly the way it sounds. Your marketing team is constantly running, running, running, and never seeing much of a change in new customers, revenues, and profits. Hamster-wheel marketing wastes *energy.* The trap of hamster-wheel marketing is that it gets you thinking that sheer energy will move your business forward.

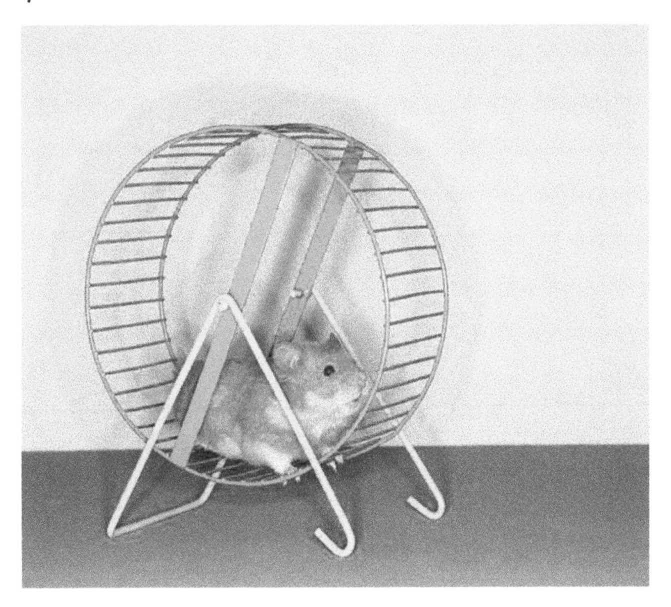

Lottery Marketing. When you're playing lottery marketing, you keep putting in the coins and pulling the lever on every new marketing idea. And it works just like in the casino, providing you with a "win" often enough to keep you wedded to the lever. Lottery marketing wastes *money.*

Shiny Ball Syndrome Marketing. This is just a brighter name for trial-and-error decision-making. It means constantly changing goals to chase every shiny new ball of potential. It wastes *time* because you are always looking for the next big thing or buying a quick fix on impulse.

Fire, Ready, Aim Marketing. You take a shot at a program or project and see if it worked; if it does not, you aim in a different direction. This approach wastes the *tools* you need to market effectively. If one shotgun doesn't work, you try another. Then another and another and another.

Make-It-Happen Marketing. You know you are engaged in make-it-happen marketing when you bark those words at your team and they know that regardless of the time, resource constraints, and personal sacrifice required, they must repeatedly pull a rabbit out of a hat and deliver on the impossible. Until they don't. They quit instead. Make-it-happen marketing wastes *talent*, the people you count on to help you grow your business.

Figure 1: Five Growth Killers

FIVE GROWTH KILLERS

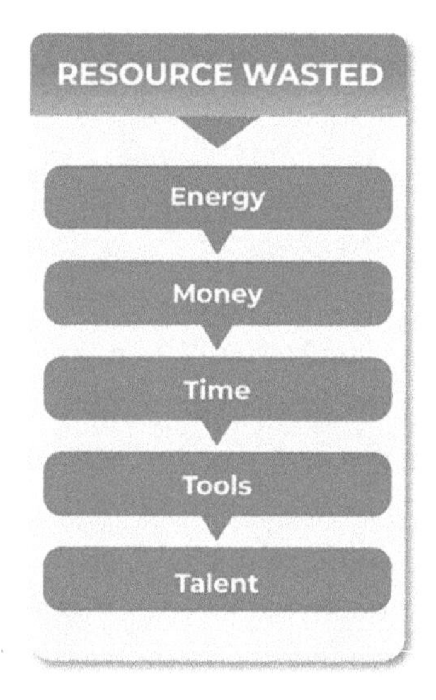

No matter which of these growth myths you buy into, the end result is the same: you are running your business in crisis management mode.

Engaging in crisis management is painful and costly on so many levels:

- The customer cost. When your organization is struggling, it creates customer churn. Customer lifetime value can be reduced by 50 percent or more as customer service declines.
- The profitability cost. Crisis management almost always results in budget-busting project cost overruns, reduced margins, revenue, and profits.
- The people cost. Top talent leaves when they are overworked, frustrated, and underappreciated working in a chaotic environment. A study by the National Association of Colleges and Employers notes that hiring an employee in a company with up to five hundred people costs an average of $7,645.[1]

But it's not just hard dollars. When talented people leave, they take knowledge, experience, and customer goodwill out the door with them.

Crisis Management Is Fun—Until It Isn't

I'll step up and admit it. I know the penalties of crisis management first-hand. I was my own worst enemy because I was addicted to crisis management. Yep, I said it. It's out there. I didn't run from crisis management. I reveled in it. It was the drumbeat of my life, and not just my working life.

Crisis management was how I ran my projects, my teams, even my friendships. Never get it done until the last minute. Make decisions in the heat of the moment, when the flames were licking my toes, because I was the boss, and I could trust my gut. It felt good to pull things out of the fire and get it done. It wasn't until later that I learned crisis management has a cost. A very deep and personal one.

One day, I was in typical crisis-management firefighting mode, rushing to meet an urgent day-of-delivery deadline that, by the way, I'd known about for three months. That day, my business partner of three years, my creative genius who helped me launch the company and build the brand, knocked on my door and said, "We need to talk."

Hard swallow. "Okay," I said. She explained to me that the company's constant churn had taken a physical toll. She wasn't just burned out; she was physically sick and needed to leave because her health was at risk.

To say that was the biggest wake-up call of my life *is an understatement*. She took a six-month leave of absence and I set about changing the way I ran the company, starting with having heart-to-heart talks with my other employees and vendors. What I learned opened my eyes to a new way of operating my company. I discovered a different way of making decisions and implementing them that eventually led to the development of the Octain Growth System (OGS).

What About You?

Think about it for a minute. What's your process for achieving your growth vision, goals, and plans? If you're like most of my clients, I'll bet you've struggled through your share of crisis-management moments, crossed-fingers guesswork, and "assess and pivot" top spinning—especially during the COVID-19 pandemic.

And yes, *I hear you*. How do you plan for the unanticipated like a worldwide pandemic? I believe the answer is not with a traditional plan.

Those CEOs who best weathered the COVID-19 storm had a framework and structures, a system in place that allowed them to be resilient and forward thinking, even flexible, in the face of the ever-changing dynamics of the pandemic response.

Traditional business planning has been dying for years. COVID-19 drove a stake through its heart. We have entered a paradigm shift and the global workplace will never be the same.

In my first book, *Make Remote Work*,[2] I highlighted the changes leaders need to address in managing people for remote and hybrid work environments; improving processes and efficiencies by moving business functions and operations to the cloud; and how to design your marketing engine for the modern remote economy.

Take Control

The solution to sustainable growth in an ever-changing, remote-led economic environment isn't better planning. The solution is an operating system that supports and energizes your business functions, an operating system that lays a foundation and enables your business to run smoothly. With an operating system in place, you can even manage through unpredictable change.

Since early 2010, I've been developing, refining, and proving my marketing operating system, the OGS, with more than three hundred companies in twenty-two different industries. That's more than forty thousand hours of hands-on, deep-dive experience in solving real-world business problems and delivering sustainable, long-term growth for small and medium-sized businesses. My clients have included businesses in technology, software as a service (SaaS), manufacturing, healthcare, transportation, financial services, and many more industries.

In each case, we used the methodology, processes, and tools of the OGS outlined in this book to deliver revenue increases from 27 to 197 percent. One client, LCS Technologies, had a three-year growth increase of 2,800 percent and landed at the top of the *INC.* 500 fastest-growth company list two years in a row.

These results come from taking control of your marketing. For most small and medium-sized businesses, marketing is something of a black hole or a magic trick: confusing, time consuming, and expensive.

Too often it's a drain on time, people, and resources that produces unpredictable results. That's why too many business owners and marketing directors resort to the trial-and-error tactics and crisis management that they hope, fingers crossed, will ultimately lead to growth.

How would it feel to take on new challenges, set new goals, and know with certainty you had the resources, the team, the time, and a GPS-quality marketing operating system you could follow to achieve your growth dreams? What would it feel like for your team to have ultimate confidence in you as a CEO, CMO, or marketing leader with no qualms about the direction you wanted them to take?

If you're ready to leave crisis-management, trial-and-error decision-making behind and enthusiastically take your business in a new direction and see better results than you've had before, dive in and let's get started. Let's explore the OGS.

Chapter 2:

WHY EXECUTION MATTERS: THE OCTAIN GROWTH SYSTEM

Sometimes all it takes is one event, or in my case, one client, to crystallize the idea and start the germination process of a new product. The OGS really came together with my client Frank Denning.

Prior to 2010, I'd been using parts of the OGS process and developed many of the tools as needed. I had a bunch of fragments of marketing "colored glass." After working with Denning, it became a mosaic.

A New Reality For Denning Packaging

"Growth! We are all about growth here." Denning was emphatic, and why shouldn't he be? The company had been in business for twenty years and had grown at least 10 percent every year except the last two.

"How has growth been the last two years?" I asked him.

"Flat as a pancake," he grunted. Denning hadn't been idle in those two years. He'd tried just about everything you'd expect an experienced, action-oriented CEO to do. He'd hired and fired three sales directors. He changed marketing strategies every few months. He'd brought in consultants to look at products, process, systems, and people, but so far nothing had worked.

Growth was still flat. Denning was running out of options and running out of time. The board was breathing down his neck. If he didn't turn things around in the next six months, he was out on his ear and he knew it.

The look in his eyes was pleading. He was a strong man, a big man. Pleading didn't come easy to him and neither did the words, "I really need your help."

"That's what I'm here for," I replied.

"You came highly recommended. Jeff at Interwind told me great things about you. So," he paused and gave me a searching look. "I have high hopes."

Hope being the operative word, I thought.

"So tell me," he continued. "Why do you think you can change things here when none of us have been able to? We've tried a few other consultants. Did their goal-setting exercises and vision boards. Strategic planning sessions and teambuilding off-site events."

He shrugged. "We followed their advice. Got a temporary revenue bump. Saw it disappear in the next quarter. Nothing long-lasting or sustainable. Now, here we are again."

He gave me an appraising glance. Challenge crowded out the pleading look of a few minutes ago.

So I asked him.

"When you get recommendations from your team or another advisor, what do you do with them?"

He looked askance, like maybe Jeff had steered him wrong. "We start working on them, of course."

"How?" I asked.

Denning shifted in his chair. I could feel the heat in the room. I'd been here before. I wasn't worried. I waited him out.

"We get our department heads together, discuss our next moves, and start executing."

"So, everyone takes their own plan of attack."

"Yeah. Sure. And we hold weekly check-ins to make sure everyone stays on the same page."

"And do they?" I asked.

Denning glanced around his office, and then looked back at me. He shook his head.

"And what about resolving conflict between ideas?"

Another shrug. "We work it out."

"With winners and losers," I finished for him and got no argument.

"I've been there too," I said. "With my own company. And I found that often there's a huge gap between strategy—strategic big-picture thinking—and tactical implementation. We close the gap between strategy and tactics. We bridge that gap with a road map that takes you and your team step by step from your current situation to your goals in a way that eliminates conflict and crisis management and creates collaborative teams all moving in the same direction."

"Nice work if you can get it," Denning said.

"It took a while. We built it over many years, working with more than two hundred companies in twenty-two different vertical markets.

"Basically, we looked at tactics as if they were strategies, and that lead to the creation of the Octain Growth System. It's a marketing operating system for accelerating revenue growth in three steps. First, we discover your growth potential. Second, we develop a road map to get you from your current location to your destination: your profit, productivity, and efficiency goals. Third, we give you a vehicle to get there by automating your business processes."

Denning nodded, thoughtful. Then he leaned forward, a gleam in his eye.

"Let's do this," he said.

In the next eighteen months, Denning Packaging instituted OGS. We discovered its current customer base was saturated with product and competition. The company needed to find a new market for its products. Finding a new geographic niche changed its competitive position and drove new sales growth of 24 percent in the first year.

> ***"Octain helped us develop a strategic launch plan that resulted in opening a new geographic market, changed our competitive position, and drove new sales growth of 24 percent in the first year."***
>
> —Frank Denning, Denning Packaging

Like Denning's team, when you follow the crisis management "make it happen" method for executing on your plan or strategy, your team typically does what they know how to do best, the tried-and-true, the comfortable. When they need to power up, they double down on harder work and longer hours. That's a recipe for burnout, not successful execution.

Planning: The Antithesis Of High Growth

If crisis management is the disease, planning must be the cure, right? Well, maybe. If the COVID-19 pandemic taught us anything, it taught us that even well-designed plans can only take us so far. Business plans, strategic plans, marketing plans—the response to COVID-19 tossed them all up in the air like so much confetti.

Traditional business and strategic plans offer goals and desired outcomes. Few deal with the everyday reality and the step-by-step journey between where the company is today, the current realities, and the desired/anticipated goal.

The scenario goes something like this: the team spends the day at an off-site event creating goals, imagining possibilities, engaging in some good invigorating blue-sky thinking. Issues get put on the table, and goals, directives, and key performance indicators (KPIs) are established. Voila, *the plan*!

At the end of the day, the CEO/CMO says, "Great session guys. Let's get it done." Everyone darts off to their respective departments and starts doing whatever activities they do best. Because there is usually little discussion of the specific actions the team will take to get to the goal from the destination, *the plan* often ends up being ignored in the rush to get stuff done.

Move Beyond The Plan

Consider what could result if your business or marketing department had an operating system instead of *the plan*. Think about having a process and set of instructions for business growth operation that provide a foundation and framework that could move the business forward, are flexible enough to anticipate change, and enable the kind of agile decision-making today's dynamic market conditions demand.

Like any good operating system, it would establish the current capabilities and the desired operational goals. It would execute according to the *rules of the road*, effectively and efficiently managing resources.

Introducing The Octain Growth System

That operating system does exist. It's the Octain Growth System (OGS), a system that will enable you to obtain growth by getting control of the one function in your organization that has the most potential to increase revenue or cost you thousands of dollars and wasted time and energy: your marketing.

The OGS has three key components:

1. Strategy. You will develop a customized strategy to create sustainable revenues, profitability, and efficiencies for your organization. This strategy is your blueprint for growth.
2. Smart execution. You will be able to develop a process and system for execution that eliminates crisis management and enables you to confidently predict return on investment (ROI). Smart execution delivers a road map to get you from your goals to your destination.
3. Automation. You will replace manual, old-school methods of working with automated systems that will increase the productivity and performance of your marketing, sales, and customer service teams.

Figure 2: OGS In Motion

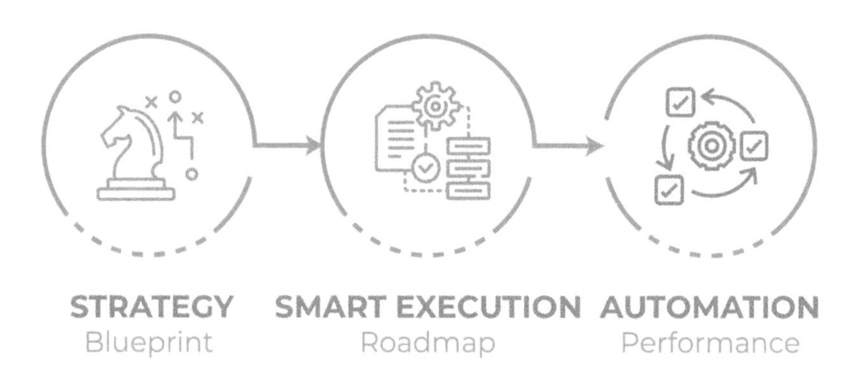

The building blocks of the OGS are six growth accelerators.

Figure 3: Meet The Accelerators

The 6 Accelerators of OGS

Here are the six accelerators of the OGS:

1. Brand development enables you to build brand awareness to become an industry or market leader.
2. Customer acquisition builds your lead generation engine by enabling you to reach more high-value customers who value and are motivated to buy your products and services.
3. Message clarity ensures that when you connect with the right prospects you have a message that connects to and engages your prospects, and converts them to customers and raving fans.
4. Market expansion enables you to increase the size of your market opportunity by showing you how to develop demand and lead-generation programs with proven micro-strategies and tactics that range from traditional to digital and social media.
5. Sales enablement improves sales effectiveness by streamlining your sales process and helping you shorten your

sales cycle through the effective alignment between marketing and sales teams.

6. Product/service innovation shows you how to improve, extend, or innovate your product to maximize your market and competitive position.

OGS uses a discovery process to turn these six functional areas into active ingredients for revenue growth. Think of the discovery process as a way to identify your current location and set your destination so you can create a road map to get you there in the second component of the OGS: smart execution.

Smart Execution: Your Road Map

What makes execution "smart"? Put simply, it means examining and evaluating the alternatives via a proven process before acting, so you know the path you are on is the right one for your project, program, and team.

And no, that doesn't mean spending days, weeks, or months building models and analyzing different alternatives before you move. It's a very simple and easy to use decision framework that will enable you to build, and have confidence in, the road map your team is using to move forward. In the case of my medical device client, it took six one-hour meetings, and we knew the best path forward.

Smart execution enables you to create a road map that delivers growth in a systematic, predictable fashion.

Imagine driving across country and never having to stop to ask for directions. That was the promise AT&T made in its series of ads in 1994 introducing the benefits of the internet. It was, as we know now, talking about a GPS. Today, few of us would consider going anywhere new without that tool.

Our GPS got a real workout when we made the move from Sacramento, California, to Raleigh, North Carolina, in 2020. It was quite the adventure, especially during a global pandemic.

Our first big decision was how to tackle the trip. Should we just get in the car, drive, and stop when we get tired? The drive-by-the-seat-of-your-pants method? Should we plan our route in advance? And if so, which route should we take?

There are lots of ways to drive across country from one coast to the other. Here are some popular options culled from the moving site U-Pack.

Figure 4: 11 Classic Cross-Country Road Trips

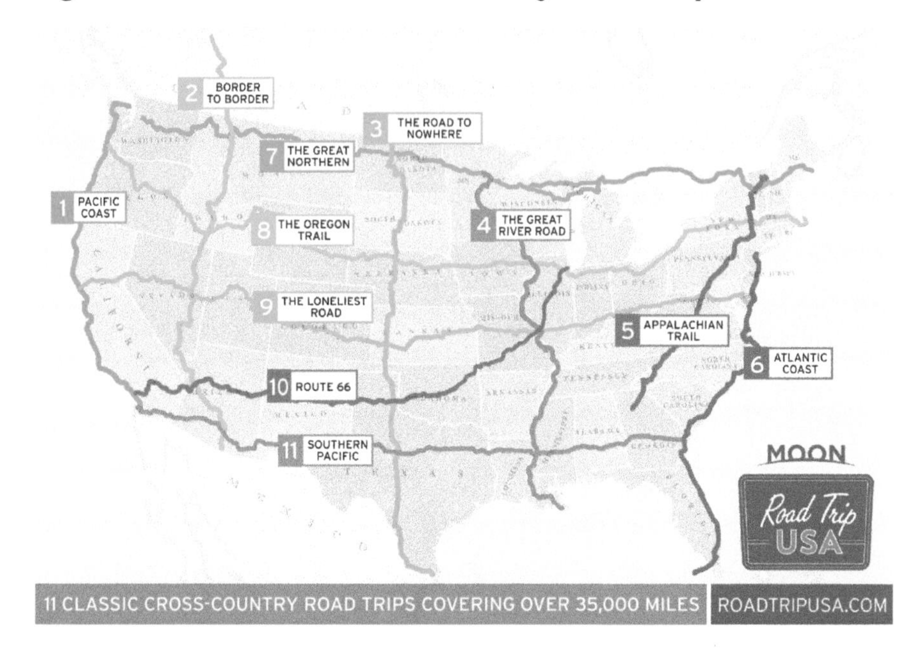

If you are looking for the shortest route, take Interstate 10. It's the shortest cross-country drive at 2,460 miles from west coast to east coast, taking you from Santa Monica, California, to Jacksonville, Florida.

Or if you like mountain driving, you can explore a northern route like I-90, going from Boston to Seattle. This route is also great for sports lovers. It's nicknamed the Hall of Fame Highway because the eastern leg has over fifteen sports halls of fame and museums within an hour of it.

Interested in fall foliage? The foliage is fantastic on US Route 50, which takes you through some prime leaf-peeping in New England and wide-open views of the mountains in Nevada.

If you want quirky attractions and photo-worthy stops, I-70 is excellent. It winds through stretches in the Midwest where there are nearby sights like the largest ball of twine (in Cawker City, Kansas).

For our trip from Sacramento to Raleigh, we chose the Southern Pacific route through Arizona, New Mexico, Arkansas, Alabama, then picked up the Appalachian Trail route to North Carolina. We wanted to visit a few vacation sites like Sedona, Arizona, and the U.S. Space and Rocket Center in Huntsville, Alabama, and we had to be in Raleigh in a week to get ready for the van to arrive.

Our cross-country road trip was an example of smart execution in action.

Automation: Your Vehicle For The Speed of Business

Today, the speed of business relies on a digital infrastructure. Automation is the vehicle that allows you to improve marketing efficiencies.

In its 2021 State of Business Automation report,[3] Zapier noted that 88 percent of small and medium-sized businesses (SMBs) said automation allowed them to compete effectively against larger competitors. The survey said that "63 percent of SMBs say automation allowed their company to quickly pivot as a result of the pandemic—whether it was bringing their goods and services online or changing their business model completely."

Despite these peer-reported advantages, most small and medium-sized businesses are behind the curve when it comes to automation. They may be dabblers with one application in one area or that is being used in one department. They may be holdouts over concerns of the cost, time, and business disruption involved.

Bring Your Business To The Cloud

Profitability and sustainable growth in the remote economy demand a digital transformation to cloud-based operations. Those who do this will gain operational efficiencies and cost reductions that will protect them through the ups and downs of any business environment. In short, you will be more than ready for the next recession or pandemic.

Figure 5: Cloud Computing

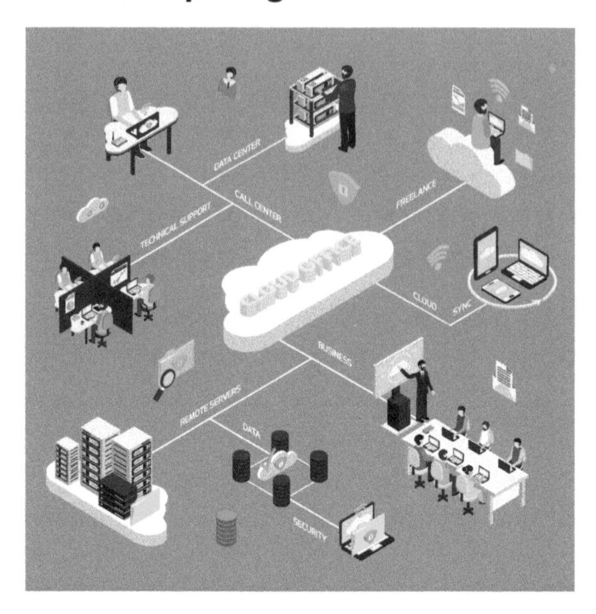

Reduce Costs, Improve Efficiencies

Driving down costs and driving up margins is a core goal of any CEO or CMO. Automation enables companies to achieve efficiencies such as those noted in figure 6.

Figure 6: Improve Efficiencies With Cloud Computing

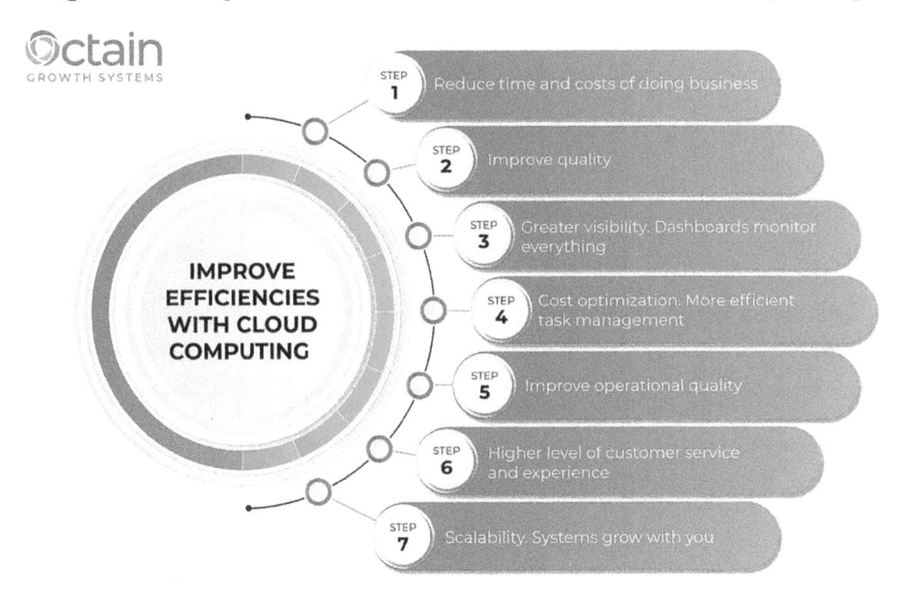

And the benefits don't stop there. Automation makes employees happier and more productive. When repetitive, time-consuming tasks are eliminated, employees are free to do the kind of work that expands their energy and creativity.

According to PwC's 2021 US Cloud Business Survey, "76 percent of business leaders are engaged in cloud strategy and 56 percent see cloud as a strategic platform for growth and innovation. PwC's survey makes it clear that cloud will be the next competitive frontier. Don't just tie cloud to your business strategy; make it the change agent that can secure your future."[4]

Move your business to the cloud. Product development. Manufacturing. Operations. Marketing. Sales. It all works in the cloud.

Chart 1: The Octain Growth System Model

Here is a quick overview summary of the Octain Growth System Model that provides the foundation for smart marketing execution.

STRATEGY	EXECUTION	AUTOMATION
Each seven-step canvas provides the strategy, goals and action steps for accelerated growth.	*Key implementation elements needed to achieve the strategic goals for that growth accelerator.*	*Baseline technology and tools required to implement and facilitate growth.*
Brand Canvas & Toolbox	Logo, fonts & colors; brand guide, PPT template, Word template, email signature.	NA
Customer Canvas & Toolbox	Customer personas; customer segments; buyers journey map.	CRM, Marketing Automation, lead generation funnel – Quiz, Click.
Message Canvas & Toolbox	Messaging plan; content fundamentals: email, blog, social posts, intro corporate and product/service videos. Canvas development will determine product choices in these areas.	Website/CMS; email marketing platform, social marketing platform.
Marketing Canvas & Toolbox	Marketing collateral, campaigns, events, advertising, resource allocation. Canvas development will determine product choices in these areas.	CRM, Marketing Automation, collaboration/ productivity platform, SEO/SEM platforms, analytics
Sales Canvas & Toolbox	Enablement team, sales process development (SLAs), success metrics, resource allocation.	Appointment/ Calendar, proposal software, enablement/ engagement platform, analytics.
Product Canvas & Toolbox	Strength evaluator, improvement worksheet, mind map, development roadmap.	Product development software.

This combination of strategy, smart execution, and automation will change the way you run your marketing, sales, and customer service departments.

PART II:

OCTAIN GROWTH ACCELERATORS

Chapter 3
BRAND DEVELOPMENT

A brand is a living entity—and it is enriched or undermined cumulatively over time, the product of a thousand small gestures.—Michael Eisner, CEO, Disney

WHO DOESN'T WANT to stand out in the crowd? What CEO or CMO doesn't want to leapfrog the competition and be number one in their market?

And the best way to do that is with a strong brand. Brands have real power. They have customer power. They have market power. They have financial power.

> ***"If this business were to be split up, I would be glad to take the brands, trademarks, and goodwill, and you could have all the bricks and mortar—and I would fare better than you."***
>
> —John Stuart, Chairman, Quaker Oats

Brand Power: Get Yours

Brands have the power to turn a struggling business into one of the strongest players in its market. A strong brand identity can help a small business compete head-to-head with more established companies. Effective brand promotion can help a growing practice attract more high-paying clients.

The Danger Of Ignoring Your Brand

Don't make the mistake of thinking you need a big Hollywood or Broadway budget to develop a brand. You have a brand. You just may not be using its power as effectively as you could be.

Everything you put in front of a potential customer—from your business card to your website—produces an impression about you, your business, and your products and services. With each impression, your customer decides whether or not they want to do business with you.

When you focus on your brand, you are simply helping that customer see you as you want them to see you, for who you are and the value you can offer to them. You help them make the right decision, to choose to do business with you and continue to do so over time.

Creating Connections, Making Memories

When most people think of a brand, they think of the visual element they see: the logo, a tagline, special colors, or a look they recognize. If the marketing team has done its job right, customers feel something about the company when they see that visual.

A brand can also be represented by a special sound, an audible brand, or even a smell, which is why you used to get perfume samples in your department store bills.

When it comes to branding, business builders know brands don't just appear. You can't develop a powerful brand by picking a logo from the internet.

Behind the scent, the sound, or the visual that represents the brand, a lot of work is done. Real brand building takes dedicated, intense effort that involves concentrated decisions about company values, customer promises, brand voice, and personality.

It is digging deep and understanding your company's *why*.

As Simon Sinek expresses it: "Every organization operates on three levels: *What* we do, *how* we do it and *why* we do it. But very few of us can clearly articulate *why* we do what we do."[5]

Brand Development

Developing a brand presence is such a daunting effort that it often gets ignored in the day-to-day effort of trying to get product out the door and new customers in.

That's why the OGS was created, built around six easy-to-use canvases. The canvas model is a snapshot of your brand on a single, at-a-glance page.

Figure 7: Octain Brand Accelerator Canvas

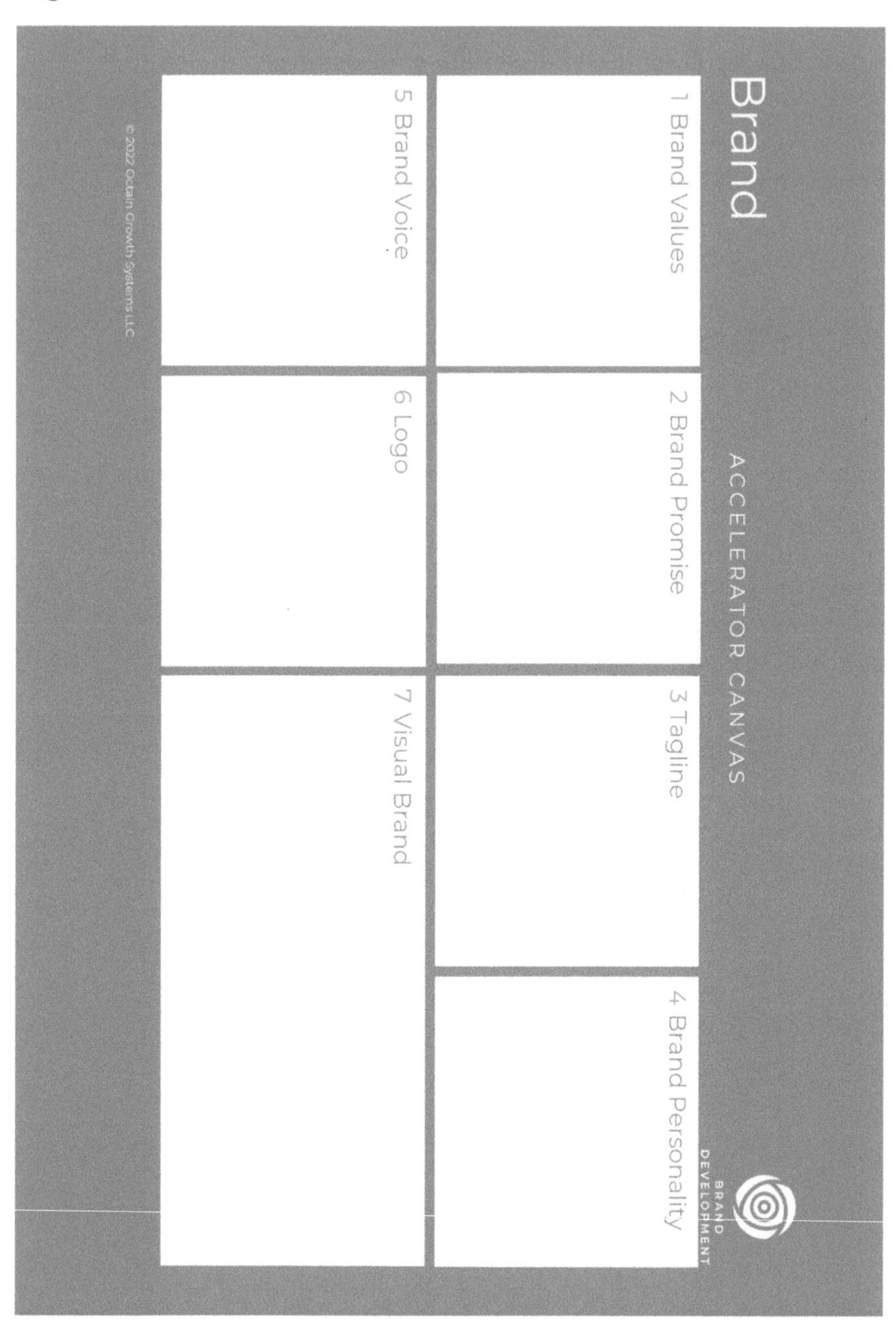

To build a strong, long-lasting brand that will stand the test of time, you must take a journey to the heart of your business and back out again. It all begins with these key components:

- *Brand Values.* Your brand values are the five to seven value words your company chooses to represent your principles, your culture, the essence of your product or service, and the behavior your employees and partners will offer to customers.
- *Brand Promise.* Your brand promise is your contract with your customer as to what you are going to give them in return for the money they are paying you. It is what your customers expect or hope to get when they buy your product and service. From the customer's perspective, the brand promise is a combination of tangible (I will get a new look) and intangible (I will feel more confident) needs, wants, and desires.
- *Tagline.* Your tagline or slogan is a short snappy statement that expresses your brand promise in an easy to remember phrase. Your brand tagline combined with your logo and your colors/typefaces is what is called your brand image.
- *Brand Voice.* This is the verbal, written expression of your brand personality used in marketing and sales materials and conversations. How will you sound to your customers and partners? From serious to quirky, every brand expresses its personality through its brand voice.
- *Brand Personality.* Your brand personality represents the image and emotion of the brand—serious, funny, predictable, quirky, your company at its best. It also reflects how you will live out your brand values with customers, employees, partners, and the marketplace.
- *Logo.* Your logo or mark is the primary visual representation of your brand. An effective logo showcases your brand values or promise. An effective logo attracts your ideal customers and gives them a sense of what it will be like to do business with you.

- *Visual Brand: Colors and Typefaces.* The colors and typefaces you choose also represent your brand values. Color influences choice and decision-making. Color psychology is so important to how people make decisions that it is the subject of intense research for communication, design, behavior modification, and attitude.[6] In marketing, color is so critical to brands that some global brands, including Sunkist, actually trademark their particular brand color.

  You build your brand brick by brick, step by step, beginning with brand values.

Step 1: Develop Your Brand Values

If people believe they share values with a company, they will stay loyal to the brand.—Howard Schultz, CEO, Starbucks

Business growth is all about providing value. Providing value to customers, employees, the market, and ultimately to the business builder and their family. In today's noisy, chaotic market, potential customers need to get the value you provide immediately. And they need to get it digitally, online.

This is something older business builders who grew up in a face-to-face sales world struggle with. By contrast, it comes naturally to digital natives or screeners, as the millennial and Gen Z generations are often called.

The rapid nature of customer decision-making makes brand development so critical. Your brand must speak to your audience for you online without your physical presence. The strength of your customer value must be clearly communicated in your brand.

Then why is brand value development so often rushed? Done in a quick meeting or two?

A typical brand development experience goes something like this. The executive and marketing team gather in the conference room. The agency team hands out a paper filled with words and asks the team to circle those that represent the company. Those words get put up on the whiteboard. Maybe twenty to thirty words are circled. Each word is discussed, debated, and ranked. In the end, five to seven words remain and voila, the brand values have been created. The final product is typically a sentence or two describing the value. And the agency is off and running, choosing colors and creating logos, mood boards, and designs. All too often, the end product strokes the egos and reflects the tastes of the marketing team but communicates virtually nothing of value to the customer.

That's why OGS does it differently. It takes a deep and detailed dive into brand value development—something it is unlikely you have experienced when working with a typical branding agency. You will notice and celebrate that difference.

New Look, New Direction

In 2019, Head Start California had a bold vision to expand services for at-risk children in California, but its old look and style was stopping that from happening. Octain's branding strategy created new branding, positioning, and messaging that has led to new recruitment and fundraising opportunities.

> *"When we started the rebranding exercise, I was dreading it. I had done this many times before with little progress. This process was completely different. It opened my eyes to a new way of thinking about our association and is leading to some significant changes in the way we position ourselves internally and externally to the community."*
>
> —Christopher Maricle, Executive Director, Head Start California.

OGS Brand Framework

Brand value development with OGS starts with a framework. Brand values are divided into three categories: one core value, three action values, and three experience values. Company value discovery begins by asking a series of key questions like these:

- *Core Value Questions.* Why did you start this business? What need or problem did you see in the market that you knew you alone could fix? Maybe you had a problem and could not find a solution, so you invented one. Or maybe you saw other people in need and knew you could help. This is the overarching motivation for your business. In branding terms, that is your *core value.*
- *Action Value Questions.* What does your company believe in that causes you to deliver your products and services in the special way you do? How do you act on those values with every customer interaction? How do you train your employees to act on these values? In branding terms, those are your *action values.*
- *Experience Value Questions.* How do your customers feel about what you do? How does your solution affect/change their life, business, relationships? How do they think, act, or respond differently in their lives and businesses because of your solution? In branding terms, those are your *experience values.*

Figure 8: Brand Value Framework

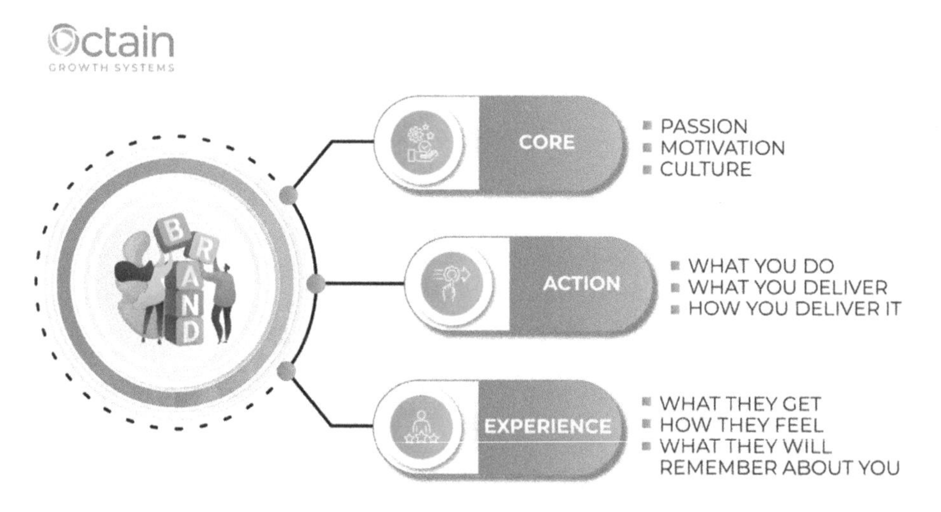

One Core Value. The core value is the fundamental value that defines and anchors the brand and the other brand values. It is the purpose of your business. If your business could only stand for one thing, one defining word, that is your core brand value. It is the essence of your brand.

Three Action Values. The action values are what your business does for your customers. Action values create the positive emotional connection with prospects that move them to action. It is these values that meet and fulfill the prospect's primary business need and motivation to buy.

Three Experience Values. The experience values are about the experience your customer has with you. These are the reasons customers keep coming back. Experience values create the context for a pleasurable, profitable, and successful transaction. They make the business transaction and personal interaction a positive, memorable experience, laying the foundation for future business opportunities and delighted client referrals.

Once you have determined the values in your business, you will have seven brand values that form the heart of your brand.

Octain Value Grid

When the talk turns to values, it is tempting to answer with the first words or phrases that pop into your head. After all, you know what you stand for, what your business represents, what is most important to you, don't you? Therefore, it is tempting to just use your initial thoughts and get it done.

The first words that pop into your head are important and need to be included in the process of choosing your brand values. But when you use the Octain value grid, you will be challenged to dig deeper and think harder about the values associated with your business.

Chart 2: Octain Value Grid

Value	Definition	What/Why	How/Example
Name the value.	Define the meaning of the word.	Explain what this value represents about your business or why it is important.	Provide an example of how you have "lived" this value in your daily work.
EXAMPLE: Growth Architect	The deviser, maker, or creator of growth in a person, thing, or organization.	The outcome is a blueprint for organizational success that leads to growth.	By helping a client define, own, and follow his vision and values, he was able to grow his company from just a few million in annual revenue to one worth over one hundred million.
Passionate (Action)	Having intense or strong feelings.	This team lives and breathes packaging solutions for customers. They love seeing their packaging displayed in the store, making products more appealing to consumers.	Longevity of time in industry; high job satisfaction of key employees and executive team.
Buying Power (Experience)	Purchasing power.	Company has the buying power to provide clients with exceptional pricing and services from a range of vendors.	Buying power that is the sum of all our clients (that equates to millions of dollars of buying power) versus just the limits of their own budget (which is almost always way less than ours). "So when we need a vendor to jump to our aid (and our client) they ask how high because they want us to be happy."

The difference between the Octain value grid and other approaches is going beyond the value word and its definition and including a *what/why statement* that showcases the importance of the value to the company/customer and a *how statement* that links a real-life example of how the value is demonstrated through action.

The Value. Values should be one to three words maximum.

The Definition Of The Value. A word can have many different uses and definitions. You should choose the definition that best explains the business use of the value and include it in the value statement so everyone on your business team sees the value the same way. A standard dictionary like Merriam-Webster's is recommended for brand definitions.

The What/Why. Why does this value fit your business and/or what does it do for the customer? This step in your brand development is critical for several reasons because it:

- provides the connection between your customers' values and motivations and your company,
- creates the foundation for the benefit statements to be developed, and
- takes the brand value from "word" to "action" in your business activities for yourself and your team.

The How. An example of how this value is being used in the business. This element of brand development is critical for several reasons because it:

- demonstrates the value in real-world situations,
- models value-based actions for employees and customers, and
- puts commitment behind the message by changing behavior.

ACTION: Complete the brand values section of the Brand Accelerator Canvas in the appendix.

Step 2: Your Brand Promise

As previously noted, your brand promise is your contract with your customers as to what you are going to give them in return for the money they are paying you. The brand promise is written as if you were speaking directly to your most valuable customers.

There are four parts to the brand promise:

1. Problem. Frames the problem you are solving.
2. Deliverable. States what the customer will actually receive in tangible goods and services, e.g., a haircut, a new car, an ebook, a coaching session.
3. Benefit. States the primary benefits of the product or service, i.e., what it will do for the customer.
4. Value. States the value of what you are offering, i.e., why it is important to the customer's life or business.

Brand Promise Example #1

Let's look at the brand promise for a manufacturing company.

Need a new or unique packaging solution? Look no further than manufacturing company. Our passionate, customer-driven team of design and engineering experts will handcraft a singularly unique custom package solution to display and deliver goods for your bakery, deli, confectionery, and other food service needs. We revel in the design challenges other manufacturers will not tackle using pressure and vacuum thermoforming.

Customer needs drive everything we do. That means we will never fit your product into what we have in stock. Instead, we will innovate to ensure you get the best performance and value in the packaging industry. You can rely on us to deliver for your thermoformed packaging needs.

1. Problem: Restaurant needed to find a unique way to display and deliver food items for sale or takeout.

2. Deliverable: Handcrafted, singularly unique custom package solution for your bakery, deli, confectionery, and other food service needs.
3. Benefit: You can rely on us to deliver for your thermoformed packaging needs.
4. Value: We will never fit your product into what we have in stock. Instead, we will innovate to ensure you get the best performance and value in the packaging industry.

Brand Promise Example #2

Let's look at the brand promise for an insurance broker.

Broker knows how highly you value financial security—especially when it comes to contemplating the kind of retirement you've dreamed about and worked hard to achieve. That's why he researches your needs and provides advice custom-tailored to your situation. He dedicates his talent, energy, intelligence, and professional skill to helping you maximize your assets so you can enjoy a lifestyle that rewards your efforts while creating well-deserved peace of mind.

1. Problem: Broker knows how highly you value financial security—especially when it comes to contemplating the kind of retirement you've dreamed about and worked hard to achieve.
2. Deliverable: That's why he researches your needs and provides advice custom-tailored to your situation.
3. Benefit: He dedicates his talent, energy, intelligence, and professional skill to helping you maximize your assets.
4. Value: You can enjoy a lifestyle that rewards your efforts while creating well-deserved peace of mind.

ACTION: Complete the brand promise section of the Brand Accelerator Canvas in the appendix.

Step 3: Your Slogan Or Tagline

A tagline or slogan is a single phrase of seven words or less that expresses a major thought about your brand. A tagline can explain a value, sum up a customer experience, or point your customer toward a feature or benefit of your product or service.

We will look at five elements to decide the best tagline for your business:

1. Value. What is the primary value you want your tagline to express?
2. Customer experience. What is the primary experience you want your tagline to express?
3. Feature. What is the most important thing you offer your customers?
4. Benefit. What is the most important thing you do for your customers?
5. Customer/tribe. Who are you connecting with?

Elements one through four are often part of the actual tagline. Element five, customer or tribe, may not be part of the actual tagline or is often expressed as "you." Don't be fooled, professional tagline writers know exactly who "you" are and exactly what "you" want when they create their taglines.

When you create a tagline for your business you need to know exactly who you are talking to as well. Here's how that works with some global brands.

- The Ultimate Driving Machine—BMW
    - expresses the *value* of BMW's German engineering
    - ultimate: the level of *experience*
    - driving machine: *feature/benefit*
- Your World. Delivered—AT&T
    - expresses the *benefit* of choosing AT&T

    - your world: the customer *experience*
    - delivered: *feature/benefit*
- The Magic Begins Here—Disneyland
    - magic: the customer *experience* of being there
    - begins here: expresses the unique *benefit* and *value* of visiting the park

As you can see, your tagline can express many different things: value, experience, feature, and benefit. All of it in just a few words. You'll notice none of these well-known taglines are more than four words.

Take a moment to review those examples, then fill in your answers below.

My value is ____
My customer experience is ______________________________
My feature is ____
My benefit is ____
My customer/tribe is ___________________________________

Now that you have the elements needed for your tagline, let's create the actual phrase.

Tagline Development

We recommend putting three to five taglines on the page and reviewing them with your team, your partners, a mastermind group, or a few of your best customers to do a little market testing before making a final decision.

You should also consider checking to see if your preferred tagline is available as a URL or domain name. It is a marketing advantage to have your company name, your product/service name (if you have one), and your tagline locked up on the internet.

Rather than just writing down the phrase, put it on a chart along with the value, features, and benefits it represents. It's a fast and easy way to capture all the elements. It looks like this:

Chart 3: Tagline Grid

TAGLINE	VALUE	FEATURE	BENEFIT	URL

Now that you've done the work and checked it with some team members, colleagues, and customers, it's time to make the big decision: choosing your memorable tagline.

ACTION: Complete the tagline section of the Brand Accelerator Canvas in the appendix.

Step 4: Your Brand Personality

Your brand personality represents the first and strongest emotion you want your prospects and customers to *feel* when they *see* your brand. It is expressed through your logo, voice, and visual image choices (colors/typestyles).

Understanding your brand personality begins with creating the emotional connection.

- *Your Emotional Connection.* Your brand personality should express your business persona and company culture. If you are a solopreneur building a personal brand around yourself, it's common to put your personality into the brand. Just express yourself, choosing visuals you like, colors that appeal to you, and typestyles that reflect your style.

- ▸ But wait. That only works if you really only want to work with people exactly like you. If you want a broader market for your products and services, you will need to consider how your potential customers connect to your brand. That's where the value work done earlier comes in.
- ▸ If you are a larger company with employees, a management team, suppliers, vendors, and established customers, your brand personality should reflect your company culture.
- ▸ Take a moment and look back at your brand Value Grid. Those values, especially your core values and your first action and experience values, were chosen by you to create an emotional connection. They should be reflected in your brand personality.

- *Your Visual Image*. This is your brand personality as represented by your visual brand: logo, colors, and typestyles. That visual connection also needs to reflect your brand values. Graphic elements, colors, and typestyles invoke specific emotions that should be considered in developing a brand personality that truly represents your brand. We'll go into more detail on developing this in step 7.
- *Your Brand Voice*. Your brand voice expresses your brand personality in the way you express your brand through the written and spoken word. The words you chose to use, how you express them, and the attitude you bring to your communication all work together to create your brand voice. Your brand voice is summed up in your slogan or tagline.

Brand Personality Example #1

Let's take a closer look at brand personality with a few examples, starting with the brand personality for Octain.

The Octain brand is about developing effective strategies to improve profitability, smart execution of those strategies to increase productivity, and automation of execution to drive operating efficiency—replacing crisis management with process and sustainability.

The emotional connection is: relief. No more crisis management and hamster-wheel marketing.

The visual connection is: strong and contemporary. It expresses quality, sophistication and intelligence as seen in the logo, below.

Figure 9: Octain Logo

- The brand voice is: clear, intelligent, and candid. It represents sophisticated knowledgeable professionalism offered with transparency and integrity.

Brand Personality Example #2

Now let's unpack the brand personality for a manufacturing company.

This brand is about a customer-driven, innovative design, and an engineering and manufacturing team that excels in developing unique, distinctive packaging that has never been done before and that takes the customers' concept to the next level of exceptional performance.

- The emotional connection is: packaging from design to delivery which gives you the freedom to create products that will delight your consumers.
- The visual connection is: the tight integration of creative problem solving and engineering design and manufacturing.
- The brand voice is: expertise, skill, and experience through creative packaging solutions.

Discover Your Brand Personality

Here is a quick way to begin the process of discovering your brand personality:

1. Review your values. What personality does each of these values exhibit?
2. Provide one personality trait for each value.
3. Pull the values together and build a character from that.
4. Express your personality as a character or avatar with common characteristics like these:
   a. Age range
   b. Occupation
   c. Interests/hobbies
   d. Personality type (consider using a profiling tool like DiSC or Enneagram as a guide)

ACTION: Complete the Brand Personality section of the Brand Accelerator Canvas.

Step 5: Express Your Brand Voice

Your brand voice expresses your brand personality through the written and spoken word. The words you chose to use, how you express them, and the attitude you bring to your communication all work together to create your brand voice. Your brand voice can be summed up in your slogan or tagline.

Here are the steps to discovering your brand voice:

1. Start with your brand personality character or avatar. Now give them a voice. What do they sound like? When they speak, what kind of language/jargon do they use? What is their speech cadence: fast, slow, moderate?

2. Review current marketing content, written and verbal, especially videos. What is the personality expressed? Does it match the brand value, promise, and tagline work?
3. Express your voice in three key words.
4. Create a brand voice chart like the one below.

Chart 4: Find Your Brand Voice

Brand Value	Personality Trait	Description	Verbal Expression
Quality	Refinement, distinction.	General excellence, mastery of standard or level; above average.	Use strong, confident words and phrases. Avoid weak or non-descript words.
Fun-loving	Light-hearted, friendly, open.	Spirited, playful, joyful.	Use open, friendly, conversational words and phrases. Avoid jargon or slang.
Passionate	Strength, intensity, enthusiastic.	Expressing, showing, or marked by intense or strong feeling.	Use strong, active words and phrases. Avoid passive words or sentence grammar.

ACTION: **Create a brand voice chart and evaluate your content against it. Revise any content that does not match your brand voice. Summarize your work on the canvas.**

Step 6: Logo

Your logo is the most important and most visible part of your brand. It is your market beacon, symbolizing who you are and what you offer to your clients and the market. It is a highly visible signal to your competitors of your reputation and market presence.

Your logo consists of three parts: color, typestyle, and graphic element. Each of these parts must come together to create the whole. The graphic element can be a shape, an icon, or a custom typeface.

Developing a logo is a critical and deliberate process that begins with considering the best way to represent your brand values, personality, and voice. Use the tools from steps 1–5 above to make sure your logo represents your values, benefits, and customer experience and not your company's product or service.

The biggest mistake business builders make is creating a logo that is a label for the product offered instead of a showcase for a benefit the customer receives.

Here's a great example of a label logo.

Dozens of carpet cleaners have a logo like this. It tells the customer the company cleans carpets but does nothing to differentiate that carpet cleaning company from any other in town.

By contrast, here is a logo for a carpet cleaning company that clearly expresses the brand personality.

And another that showcases the company's specific area of expertise—move out cleaning services—so the customer knows exactly what they do best and when to call them.

ACTION: Hire a professional graphic designer to develop your logo. The interplay between a graphic element, colors, and typestyles is subtle and takes a professional eye. It is worth the investment to get the right look for your company. Add your finished logo or logo ideas to the canvas.

Step 7: Visual Brand Identity

Your visual connection is your brand personality as represented by your visual brand: logo, colors, and typestyles. That visual connection also needs to reflect your brand values, personality, and voice.

Too often, brand development stops with the visual element. Your designer or agency hands off the graphics files and the branding guide and you're done.

Not so fast. In OGS, everything is done based on strategy and smart execution. Brand development is no exception. Your brand goes from being a symbol to being a business growth accelerator when you employ a visual communication strategy.

Developing Visual Communication Strategy

A visual communication strategy consists of three things working together in harmony: strategic focus, your visual design, and how you communicate that visual design.

Strategic focus. The faster the pace, the more important effective strategy becomes. Based on your work in the previous sections, you now have a brand strategy based on your brand values, your personality, and your brand promise. Now, you will connect that strategy to a visual look and feel.

Visual design. Compelling graphics, stunning photography, videos, multimedia, printing—our impressions of a company, brand, or person are formed first with our eyes. How your brand looks and the emotional connection that visual creates will determine your market success. Choosing wisely and with expert guidance is key to success in visual communications.

Communication. It's a noisy, fragmented world with no signs of slowing down. Where and how you choose to communicate your message can make or break your marketing campaign. From Twitter to television, across the internet, and through printed pieces, you need concise graphic design and a logo that move your audience to action.

Whether you are working with a graphic designer or choose to buy a logo online, these three things will help you make the best choices for the visual elements of your brand and create a visual communication strategy.

Once you have completed the brand canvas, it will look something like this:

Figure 10: Completed Brand Accelerator Canvas

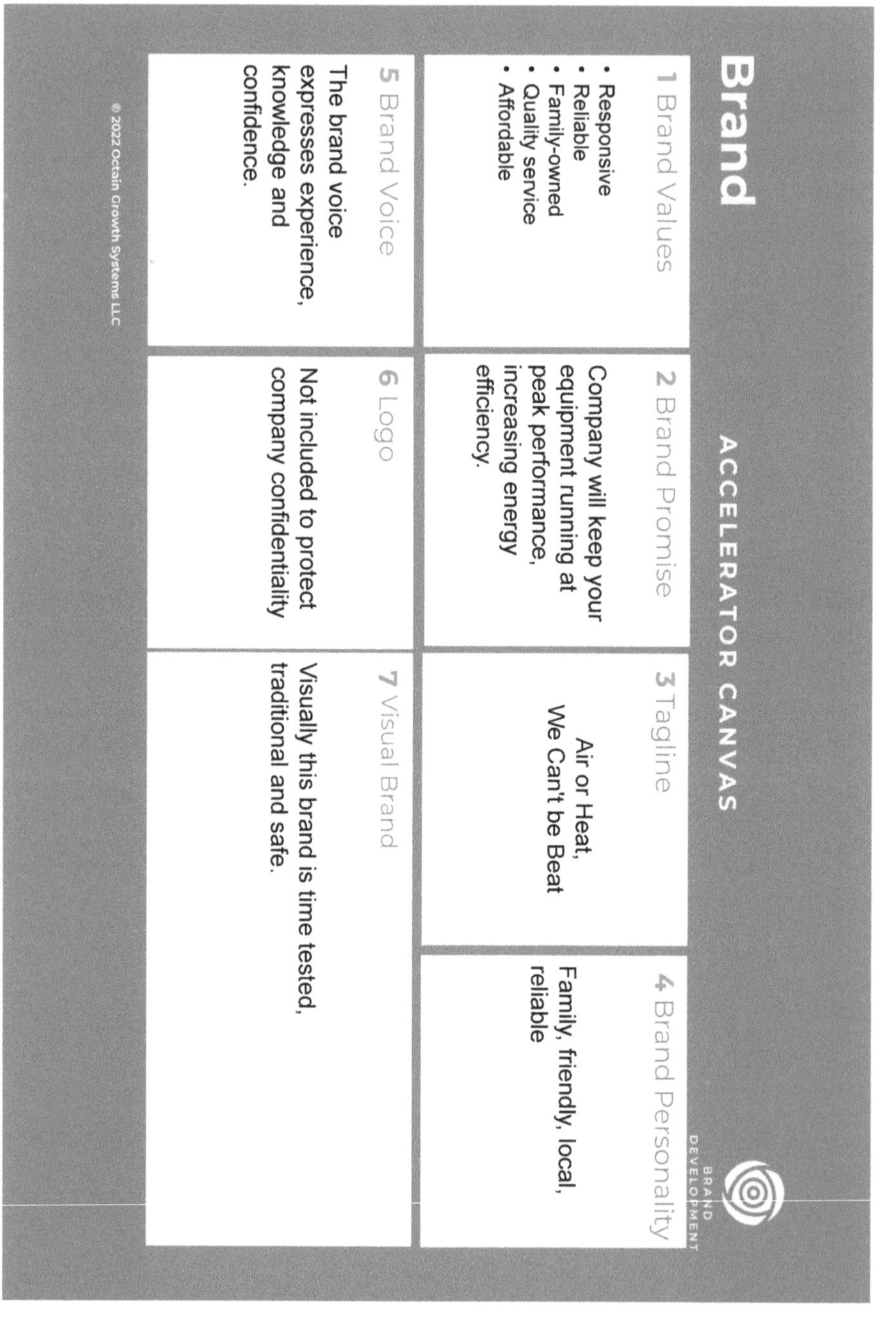
Brand
ACCELERATOR CANVAS
BRAND DEVELOPMENT
1 Brand Values
• Responsive
• Reliable
• Family-owned
• Quality service
• Affordable
2 Brand Promise
Company will keep your equipment running at peak performance, increasing energy efficiency.
3 Tagline
Air or Heat, We Can't be Beat
4 Brand Personality
Family, friendly, local, reliable
5 Brand Voice
The brand voice expresses experience, knowledge and confidence.
6 Logo
Not included to protect company confidentiality
7 Visual Brand
Visually this brand is time tested, traditional and safe.
© 2022 Octain Growth Systems LLC

Keys To Brand Acceleration

Use these action steps to get the most value from your brand value canvas:

1. Download the brand development worksheets for values, promise, tagline, and personality from the Brand Accelerator Toolbox on our website: www.octaingrowth.com.
2. Assign team members to complete the worksheets.
3. Do an off-site review to plan implementation.
4. Infuse your culture with your brand values by creating an infographic from the *why* and *how* columns of the value grid.
5. Complete the brand action guide from the Brand Accelerator Toolbox on our website: www.octaingrowth.com.
6. Refresh all your marketing elements—website, social media profiles and posts, digital ads, videos, and email signature. Include all content: brochures, product flyers, case studies, etc.
7. Reinforce your brand values in your copy to make sure you are talking about the value you offer, not just about the things you do.

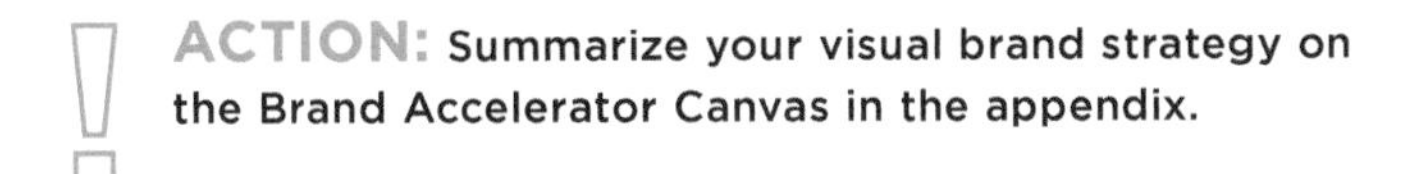
ACTION: **Summarize your visual brand strategy on the Brand Accelerator Canvas in the appendix.**

You can find more tools needed for the canvas in the OGS Brand Accelerator Toolbox on our website at www.octaingrowth.com.

Chapter 4
CUSTOMER ACQUISITION

Get closer than ever to your customers. So close that you tell them what they need well before they realize it themselves.—Steve Jobs

What Is A Customer?

IF YOU HAVE been in business very long and have attended any marketing workshops or webinars or read any marketing books, you no doubt have been told that you need to find your ideal customer.

Historically in marketing, a customer is someone who comes into your shop (online or off-line) to purchase something. They leave your shop, use your product, and come back again when they need more. It is a simple series of transactions.

The idea of transactions is so yesterday. Today, businesses and organizations are looking to form relationships with those they do business with. But those who really "get it" know that is over too.

A successful business today does not focus just on customers or even relationships.

Your business needs to focus on developing tribes, closely related groups of people, businesses, and organizations with whom you have a mutually beneficial exchange of goods and services.

Tribes matter so much in modern marketing because of social media, especially reviews. A brand can be made or broken by social excitement or social backlash. Having a tribe promoting your company/brand in social media and with social influencers is worth its weight in gold.

The value of a tribe in terms of your revenues and profits is often referred to as customer lifetime value (CLV).

CLV is a metric that estimates how much value (usually revenue or profit margin) any given customer will bring to your business over the course of the total time they interact with your brand—past, present, and future.

To calculate CLV, you need to start by multiplying the average purchase value by the average number of purchases to determine customer value. Then, once you discover the average customer lifespan, you can multiply that by customer value to determine CLV.[7]

As a rule of thumb, your CLV should be at least three times greater than your customer acquisition cost (CAC). In other words, if you're spending $10,000 on marketing to acquire a new customer, that customer should have a CLV of at least $30,000.[8]

Given the business growth benefits of CLV, it is worth investing the time, talent, money, and effort to build strong tribes of loyal fans.

Know Them Better Than They Know Themselves

To know them is to love them. More important than you knowing and loving your customers is to get your customers to love you, refer you, and buy more from you.

The Octain customer accelerator canvas is designed to help you create the blueprint for an effective customer acquisition and retention strategy by building a customer persona you can use to develop all of your marketing and sales strategies and programs.

A customer persona, also called an avatar, is a collective profile of your ideal customer based on market research and real data about your existing customers. It's called a persona or avatar when you create a real character for your marketing focus rather than a generic set of characteristics.

Meet Debi a client persona created for a financial planner.

Customer acquisition today is all about providing unique personal experiences for every customer. Personas are the secret to achieving that.

The OGS customer accelerator canvas walks you step by step through a process of discovery, decision, and action to create a customer persona you can use for all your marketing and sales efforts.

Figure 11: Octain Customer Accelerator Canvas

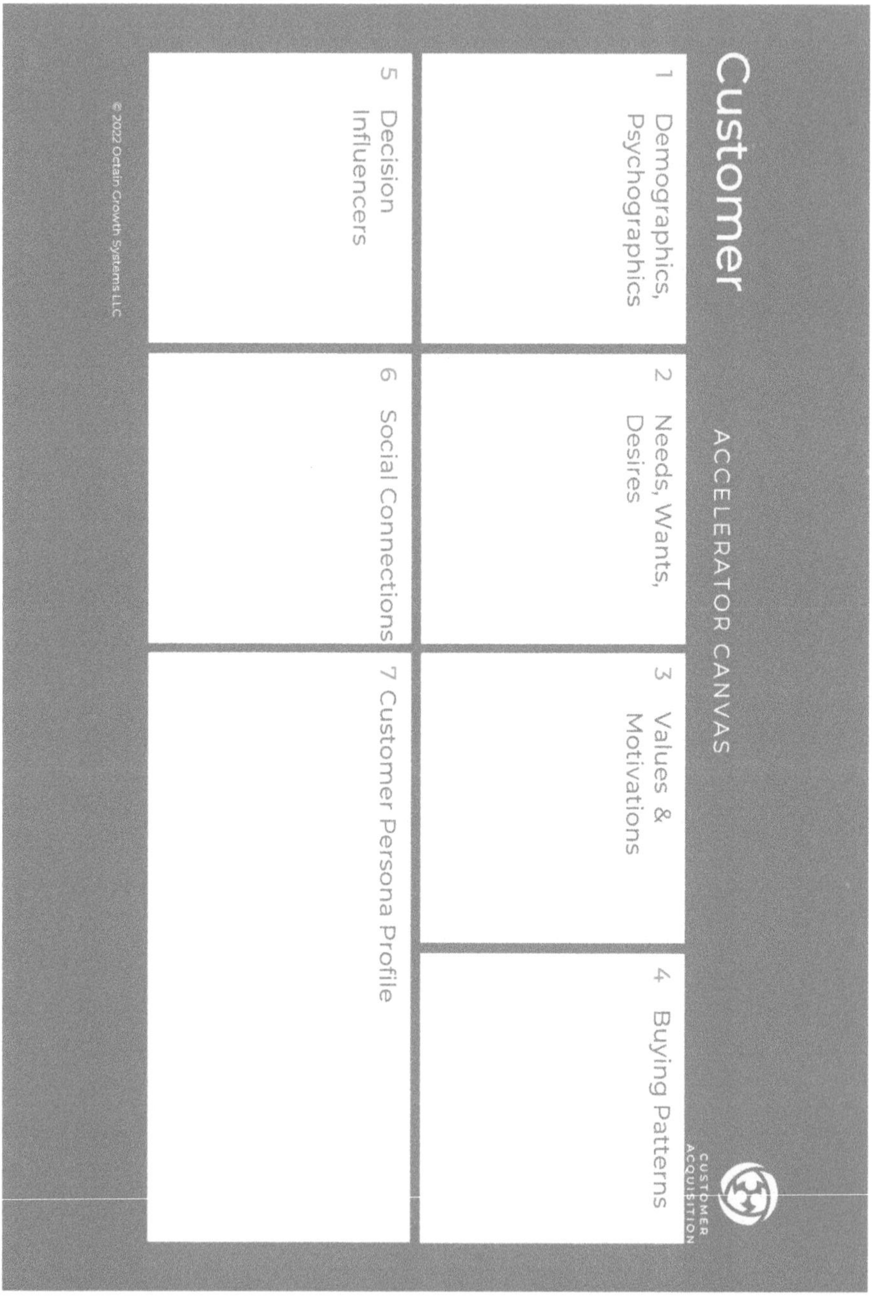
Customer
ACCELERATOR CANVAS
1 Demographics, Psychographics
2 Needs, Wants, Desires
3 Values & Motivations
4 Buying Patterns
5 Decision Influencers
6 Social Connections
7 Customer Persona Profile
CUSTOMER ACQUISITION
© 2022 Octain Growth Systems LLC

Warring Factions Eliminated

I stopped a company's internal war with this canvas. My start-up medical device client had three big customer opportunities and the resources to effectively service one. These were huge market opportunities: big pharma, big hospital networks, and physicians' networks. The problem was each of the executives wanted to serve a different market: the CEO wanted to go after big pharma; the CMO, my contact, thought hospital networks were the best bet; and the CTO was voting for physicians' networks. Because they could not agree, they did nothing. They were spinning in crisis mode and their competitors were moving in.

Using the Octain customer accelerator canvas, we mapped out the three customer personas and markets against the resources needed to win each market. During the process, it became clear to all three executives that they needed to pursue hospital networks. Once they had clear direction, they moved the company forward and they became friends again. The result was effective execution, collaboration, and a big jump in sales.

"Our team used to be all over the map trying to target the right customers. Using the customer accelerator canvas has helped us develop a focused strategy for reaching our best prospects and we have seen sales jump 40 percent in six months."—CMO, medical device manufacturer

While not all executive teams are at war when choosing a new customer target, most have conflicting ideas, recommendations, and approaches. It is a momentous decision involving significant time and resources. Getting it wrong means lost sales, market share, and profitability.

The decision to pursue a new customer segment is too important to be left to a gut decision or the loudest voice in the room.

It requires a proven process that supports decision-making with data and knowledge. That process is presented here in the Octain customer accelerator canvas.

Step 1: Understand Your Customers

Your market, often called your market niche, is the collection of people, businesses, and/or organizations that are most likely to need or want the products and services you provide. Your goal is to go from the broad to the specific—from the broad market (a huge group of possibilities) to your tribe (those with whom you can form a long-lasting connected relationship).

It's a little like peeling an onion or, my preference, an artichoke. The best part is the heart. The following questions will help you determine the general market of customers for your products and services. In this section, you are looking primarily at what is called demographic information or a demographic profile: this is the statistical characteristics of human populations (such as age or income) used to identify markets or a market (or segment of the population) identified by demographics.

The Questions That Lead To Discovery

You want to start by asking some key questions. These questions will get to the heart of the kind of customers that will value you and what you have to offer. Take time to answer them. Dig deep.

The deeper you are willing to dig at this stage, the better your answers will be and the better your results. These questions should be asked of all the stakeholders in your company who have an impact on how your company, products, and services are presented. That includes:

- your management team,
- your employees,
- your vendor and affiliate partners, and
- your top customers.

Which questions you answer depend on your primary market focus, one of the three below:

1. *Business Market.* Answer this set of questions if your products and services are primary sold to other businesses or

companies. This is commonly called B2B, i.e., business to business.

2. *Consumer Market.* Answer this set of questions if your products and services are primarily sold to people or individuals, families, couples, or people for their pets. This is commonly called B2C, i.e., business to consumer.
3. *Nonprofit.* Answer this set of questions if your products and services are offered through a nonprofit organization or agency. The questions in this section cover clients and donors/partners.

A short sample of the key questions appears below. You can download the entire survey for all three markets on our website.[9]

Discovery Questions

1. Which best describes your situation:
    a. I have lots of great customers and want more of them.
    b. I have a few great customers and want more of them.
    c. I have no customers and need to get started.
    d. I have great customers and want to expand my business into a new type of customer or geographic region.
2. I typically work or want to work with these types of companies:
    a. Public sector
    b. Private sector
    c. Non-profit sector
    d. Large companies/agencies/organizations (over a hundred employees)
    e. Mid-size companies/agencies/organizations (from twenty to a hundred employees)
    f. Small companies/agencies/organizations (under twenty employees)

3. I typically work or want to work with/in the following industries (list up to five):
    a. ______________________________
    b. ______________________________
    c. ______________________________
    d. ______________________________
    e. ______________________________
4. The companies I typically work with are:
    a. New businesses/start-ups
    b. Established (in business more than five years but less than ten)
    c. Mature (in business ten years or more)
5. The companies I typically work with are:
    a. New/launching
    b. Gaining traction (first customers)
    c. Established and/or growing
    d. Struggling
    e. Failing
6. My customers are located:
    a. Local
    b. Statewide
    c. Regional (two or more states)
    d. National
    e. International
7. My customers typically buy from me via:
    a. Direct sales
    b. Indirect sales (through a distributor, third party, or non-employee sales rep)

   c. Online
   d. Retail location (including trade show, farmers market, arts and craft show, flea market, etc.)

8. What is the typical revenue range of your preferred customer/company?
9. What is the geographical location of your preferred customer/company?
10. What percentage of your sales are done online?
11. What percentage of your sales are done in person?
12. What percentage of your sales are done at a retail location (including gym, trade show, farmers market, arts and craft show, flea market, etc.)?

Name Your Market Niches

There are riches in niches. The biggest mistake I see business builders make, especially new entrepreneurs, is trying to market to everyone. Too many business owners see customer acquisition strategies as a big circle, and they get lost in the vastness of it.

The reality is that a good customer acquisition strategy is more like a piece of pie. Start from a specific pinpoint, the tip of the pie, and expand outward to larger and larger segments as your company grows.

Where is the tip of your pie? It is in your niche market—the small section of the market you can dominate with your current resources.

Reviewing the answers to the questions above, please name your top three market niches here.

Chart 5: Riches in Niches

NICHE	GEOGRAPHY	DEMOGRAPHIC	PRODUCT FIT
Proposed target market segment	Where are they located?	What are the key characteristics of this segment?	How likely are they to value your product/service?

Chart 6 provides an example for a landscape architect.

Chart 6: Example Market Niches—Landscape Architect

NICHE	GEOGRAPHY	DEMOGRAPHIC	PRODUCT FIT
Homeowners—new construction	Sacramento	Ages 45-65, singles, married couples or with partners, one to three children, professional, white collar, upper middle class, affluent, income $100,000 and up	Extremely high and motivated to use services.
Homeowners—remodels, repairs	Sacramento	Ages 30+, maybe new homeowners, solid middle class and same as above	Motivated and also budget conscious. Need some convincing.
Power partners—custom home builders, complementary trade services	Sacramento	Established trade businesses and builders focused on remodels, upgrades, or custom-built homes	Highly motivated when part of their custom build.

ACTION: Fill out the market niche worksheet above if you have not already done so, and be sure to summarize your work on the Customer Accelerator Canvas in the appendix.

And you are done with the first step. This is where so many customer profiles and persona development stop—with demographics and niche discovery.

In the OGS, this is just the beginning. As you can see from the canvas, there are five more steps to develop your customer acquisition strategy. That means we will continue to refine your niche opportunities until you have a detailed understanding of exactly how to connect and market to this value group of prospects.

Step 2: Uncover Needs, Wants, And Desires

Early in my consulting career, I needed to learn how to sell my own services versus being the tech consultant in a global research firm or the marketing manager in a software company. It was a big transition, and I was looking everywhere for help.

One of the best resources that I found was the *Little Red Book of Selling*[10] by Jeffrey Gitomer. Later that year, I was lucky enough to attend his conference in Sacramento, where he upended one of the biggest misconceptions about understanding your customer: finding their pain.

It's common knowledge, really cliché, that you must find the customer's pain point before you can market to them or sell them anything.

Not so, says Gitomer. Here's his take:

"My insurance agent came over last week to update my portfolio of policies. I like to make sure I'm more than covered. I asked my agent (who I have been friends with, and loyal to, for fifteen years) how he engages a prospective customer.

"Well first I try to find their pain," he said with that all-knowing smile. "What!?" I screamed. "When did you learn that? 1972?

"Why aren't you trying to find positive things instead of negative things? I've been your customer for fifteen years and you never found my pain. I never had any pain. I just needed some insurance. I wasn't hurting for insurance. The only pain I had was writing you a check. In fact, that's STILL a pain."

We laughed. But "finding the pain" is not a bit funny in sales. In fact, it's somewhere between sad and manipulative. Somewhere between negative and dark. In short, if you want to find pain, become a doctor—people will come to you with pain by the thousands. If you want to make it in sales, there are other things to find. Pain does not drive a sale."

That is the exact moment I switched my customer profiling strategy to focus on uncovering needs, wants, and desires instead of pain.

- *Needs.* What problem do they need to solve? Needs can be challenges, obstacles, or even a puzzle. It might be painful. It might not be.

- *Wants.* What do they want to change about their business or life? How will changing that make them happier, more fulfilled?
- *Desires.* What do they desire to have to make their life/business better? As opposed to wants, desires can be more of a wish, a desire to have or make—something that feels far off, out of reach. Provide that to your customer and you've found the real gold in the marketing and sales opportunity.

  You uncover needs, wants, and desires with probing questions such as:

- What motivates people/businesses to work with you?
  - financial needs
  - personal improvement
  - health
  - lifestyle
  - family/relationship
  - faith/charity
- My customers are most likely to buy my product/service, when:
  - they are looking for a change;
  - they want to make an improvement;
  - they want to have fun;
  - they have a new project, person, or thing that requires my services;
  - they have to solve a problem or address a challenge;
  - they are required by law or regulation.
- My typical customers consider my product/service to be:
  - essential—can't live without it
  - important—will buy it as often as they can
  - nice to have—use occasionally
  - a necessary evil

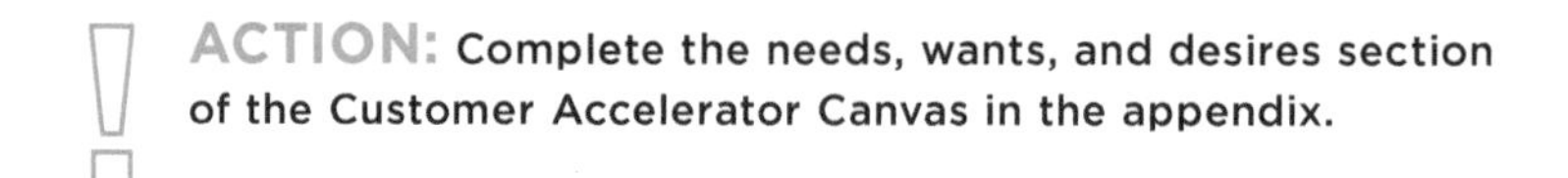

ACTION: Complete the needs, wants, and desires section of the Customer Accelerator Canvas in the appendix.

Step 3: Determine Values And Motivations

Like needs, wants, and desires, people are motivated by what they value. Today, value-based purchasing is trending, becoming, in some cases, the primary motivator for a purchasing decision.

Customers "Reimagine" Their Post-Pandemic Lives

Post-pandemic soul-searching has caused consumers across the globe to rethink and reimagine their priorities in life, including how the goods and services they buy are produced.

"Accenture's recent survey of more than 25,000 consumers across twenty-two countries notes that 50 percent of consumers say that the pandemic caused them to rethink their personal purpose and re-evaluate what's important to them in life. Forty-two percent say the pandemic made them realize they need to focus on others more than themselves. These consumers —Accenture calls them the 'Reimagined'—are changing their buying habits accordingly."[11]

The survey found that "76 percent of the Reimagined are attracted to doing business with brands that source services and materials in highly ethical ways—versus 52 percent of the traditional. Researchers also found that 65 percent of the Reimagined are attracted to doing business with brands that are environment-friendly, provide credible 'green' credentials for products/services, minimize harm on the environment and/or invest in sustainability—versus 29 percent of the traditional buyers."

With values-based buying as a framework, we can now look at motivations. People buy to achieve or acquire what they need, want, or desire most. Here are a few examples:

> Example A: If your customer *needs* to save money, they *value* the best price for their purchase and they are *motivated* by cost savings.

Example B: If your customer *desires* to lose weight, they *value* healthy living and they are *motivated* to purchase low-fat foods, an exercise program, and health supplements.

Example C: If your customer *wants* to send their child to college, they *value* education and they are *motivated* to purchase a college savings plan, college prep courses, and tutoring.

ACTION: Fill out the values and motivations grid below for up to three market niches and record them on the Customer Accelerator Canvas in the appendix.

Chart 7: Values And Motivations Grid

Customer/ Market Niche	Needs	Wants	Desires	Values	Motivators
Group 1					
Group 2					
Group 3					

Step 4: Understanding Buying Patterns

Some people are shoppers. Some are not. I am not a big shopper. When I go shopping in person or online I have a specific item or list I'm after. I get it and I'm gone. My sister, on the other hand, is a consummate shopper. She may have something in mind to buy but she is also on the lookout for a hot trend or a great deal. She will spend much more time looking before she buys. Different personalities, different buying patterns.

Buying patterns illuminate the *why* and *how* behind customer purchase decisions.

In the B2B market segment, recognizing and understanding buying patterns is extremely important because the buying dynamics are much more complex than they are in the B2C space. They involve the decision-makers (usually more than one) and a host of influencers from purchasing and department heads to policy makers within the organization like human resources.

Why Customers Buy

Three factors illustrate why customers buy goods and services:

- Urgency—How badly is the product or service needed to solve a need or want? In marketing and sales, this is often referred to as above-the-line *must-have* or below-the-line *nice to have.*
- Frequency—Is this a one-time purchase or once purchased will it be continually repurchased?
- Impact—What is the impact of the purchase on the business?
    - Routine—Always purchased, i.e., a part for a manufactured product.
    - Limited—Decision will have limited impact on the business, i.e., minor cost, short-term duration such as a product/service/operations gap requirement.
    - Major—Decision will have a major impact on the business, e.g., new building, new equipment, new hires.

- Impulse—Unexpected purchase based on a special offer, discount, or opportunity.

Figure 12: The Customer's Journey

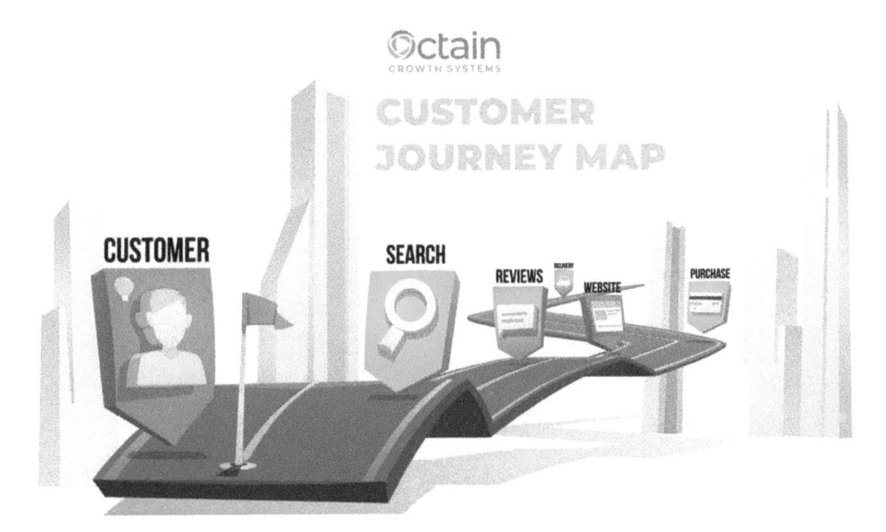

How Customers Buy

We refer to how customers buy as the buyer's journey. Put simply, the buyer's journey is the path a customer takes to get from the initial realization of the need, want, or desire to the satisfaction/resolution of that need through a purchase.

This is *big*. Whether or not you know the buyer's journey can make or break your marketing efforts. Not knowing this journey often leads to failed marketing campaigns and wasted time and money. Knowing the buyer's journey means you can put the right message/offer in front of the prospect at the right time and that's what leads to sales.

A typical buyer's journey has these stages:

- Awareness/trigger for action—We need to solve a problem.
- Discontent—What we have isn't working now.
- Need/Want/Desire—We need to find a solution.

- Consideration—What are the options/available solutions?
- Resolution—Decision time: This is what we are going to do.

At each step in the buyer's journey, the prospect takes an action to move to the next stage.

Figure 13: Buyer's Journey By Stage And Action

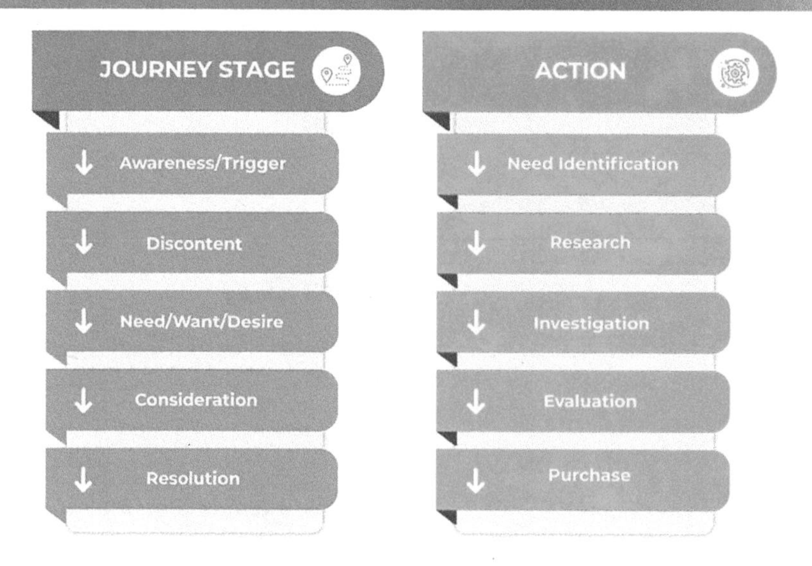

Insights and Analysis

Many digital tools exist for analyzing, understanding, and predicting buying behavior. Among the best and most popular are:

- Google Analytics
- Facebook Insights
- Analytics based on customer relationship management (CRM). Every CRM platform has some tracking analytics.

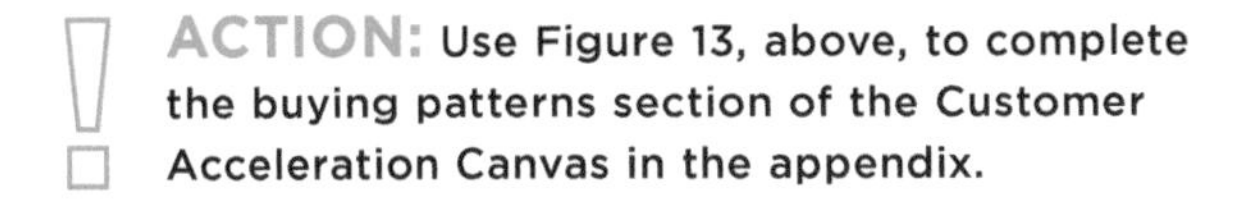

Step 5: Discovering Customer Influencers

This step of the customer accelerator canvas looks at who most influences your customers' decisions to buy.

No one decides in a vacuum. Even those who rely mostly on their gut are still influenced by circumstances, beliefs, and the world around them.

Four factors influence human decision-making:

1. Cultural
2. Social
3. Personal
4. Psychological

Much of this general information can be learned through the demographic profiles you compiled in step one. That sets the context for what influences the decision.

Within that context, you need to know who or what are the primary influencers. Those influencers can have a profound impact on whether to buy and from what company. An effective customer acquisition strategy markets both to the customer and the people and communities who most often influence or control their decision to buy. This is where understanding and connecting to your tribes becomes critically important.

Influencers can be friends, family, colleagues, competitors, or peers. They can also be paid, celebrities, or industry stars. That is its own specialty of industry marketing.

For example, a manufacturing executive is likely to be influenced internally by her management team, purchasing agent, operations director, factory floor, or warehouse manager. She might be externally influenced by her peer group of CEOs, management consultants, or what she sees and reads across the internet.

The latter is where marketing, particularly content marketing, comes into play as this chart from Marketing Charts[12] aptly illustrates.

Figure 14: Types Of Influencer Content

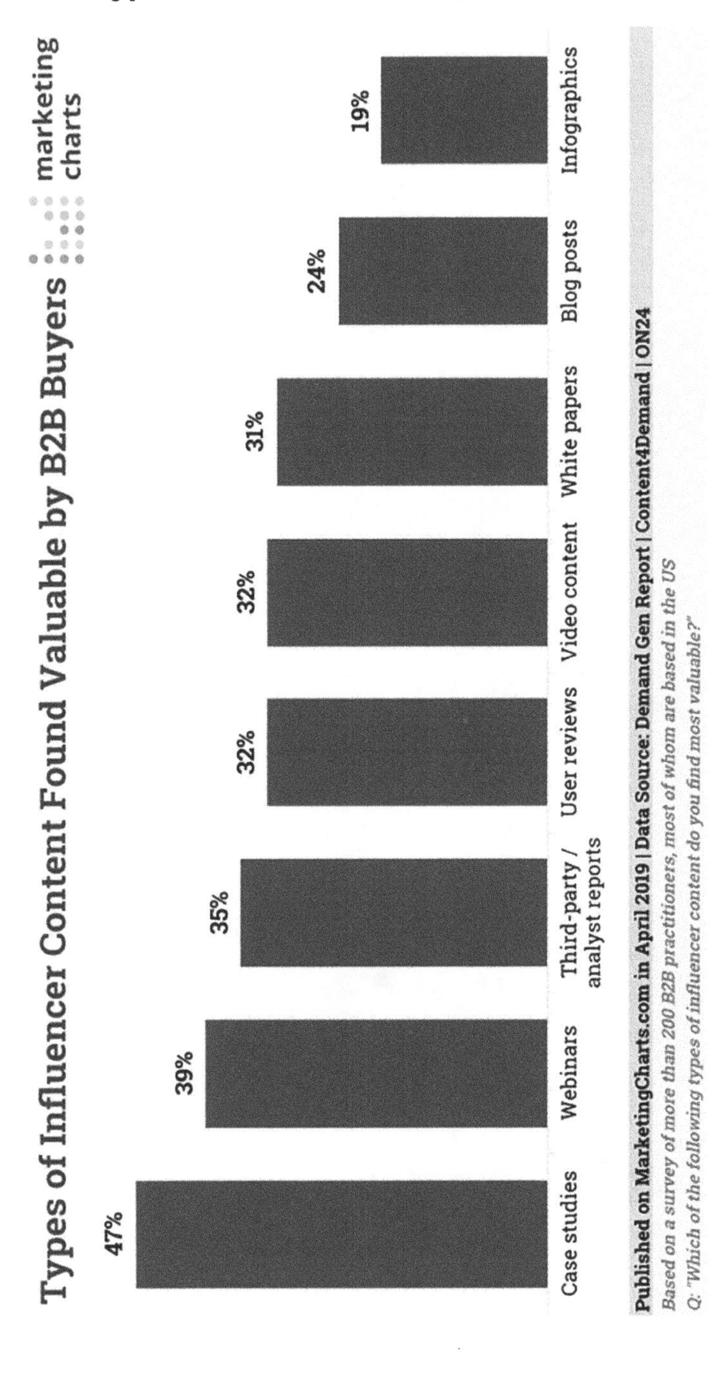

ACTION: Complete the decision influencers section of the Customer Acceleration Canvas in the appendix.

Step 6: Social Connections—Developing Tribes

Of the four factors influencing the decision-making process, one of the strongest is social connections. That includes social media, and all other social connections such as peer groups, networks, clubs and organizations, churches, and charities.

In old-school marketing, those groups were called market segments. Today, they are better known as tribes. Your tribe consists of the potential friends, fans, and followers (customers) who most need or desire what you have to offer. They are the ones with whom you can form a connection and have the best long-term relationship.

Tribes build a successful business and keep that business going when challenges such as the COVID-19 pandemic occur. Such was the case with my client, Panviva.

When the pandemic hit in 2020, Panviva, a knowledge management software company, had a choice. It could, as many did, hunker down and choose to wait out the storm. It chose a different path. Instead, the company reached out to its tribe, a loyal group of customers.

It wasn't easy because everything and everyone was in flux at the beginning of the pandemic. In fact, the company's best telemarketing person was hung up on multiple times as stressed-out customers tried to figure out how to cope with the situation. The Panviva team kept reaching out gently and sincerely and found their software solution was needed now more than ever. They had to adjust their processes and delivery, but that willingness to make the shift meant they could come back stronger than ever. A big reason for the company's success in the chaos was that it had built a loyal tribe before the pandemic and knew those customers well.

Determining Social Connections

It's simple. You want your marketing and advertising efforts to be spent where your customers will notice them. That is where they spend their time: work, family, and free time.

There are important reasons for understanding these social connections and their importance to your target customers.

- The most obvious, stated above, is to be where they are.
- Second, you can identify hidden gem marketing opportunities where real connections are made.
- Third, it is important to your messaging. Customers who belong to certain groups usually share the same values and interests. Connecting your message to those group/association values will increase engagement.

As modern marketers and business builders, we have a kneejerk reaction to focus most of our efforts on social media networks and digital advertising. That can mean we miss the hidden social connections that are smaller and offline.

One of my insurance broker clients marketed almost exclusively through the local school sports team with banners at the stadium, coupons and jerseys, digital assets (emails and social posts), and fundraisers. He was the biggest broker in that community despite heavy competition from national firms.

Chart 8: Determining Your Social Connections

In the chart below, check off your customers' social connections by customer segment. In column three rate the strength of that connection as high (5), medium (3), low (1).

Social Connections	Customer Segment #1	Customer Segment #2	Customer Segment #3	Strength (1 to 5)
Social Networks				
LinkedIn				
Facebook				
Twitter				
Instagram				
YouTube				
TikTok				
Professional Networks (Chambers, Rotary, BNI, LeTip, ProVisors, EO, ACG, XPX)				
Associations (Business, profession, industry)				
Social/athletic clubs				
Community/Faith-based				
Other				

ACTION: Use Chart 8 to determine the strengths of your tribes. Add their social connections to the Social Connections section of the Customer Accelerator Canvas.

Step 7: The Finished Profile— Your Customer Persona

Here is an example of a completed customer persona.

Figure 15: Customer Persona Example

An example of the completed customer accelerator canvas is shown on the next page.

Figure 16: Completed Customer Accelerator Canvas

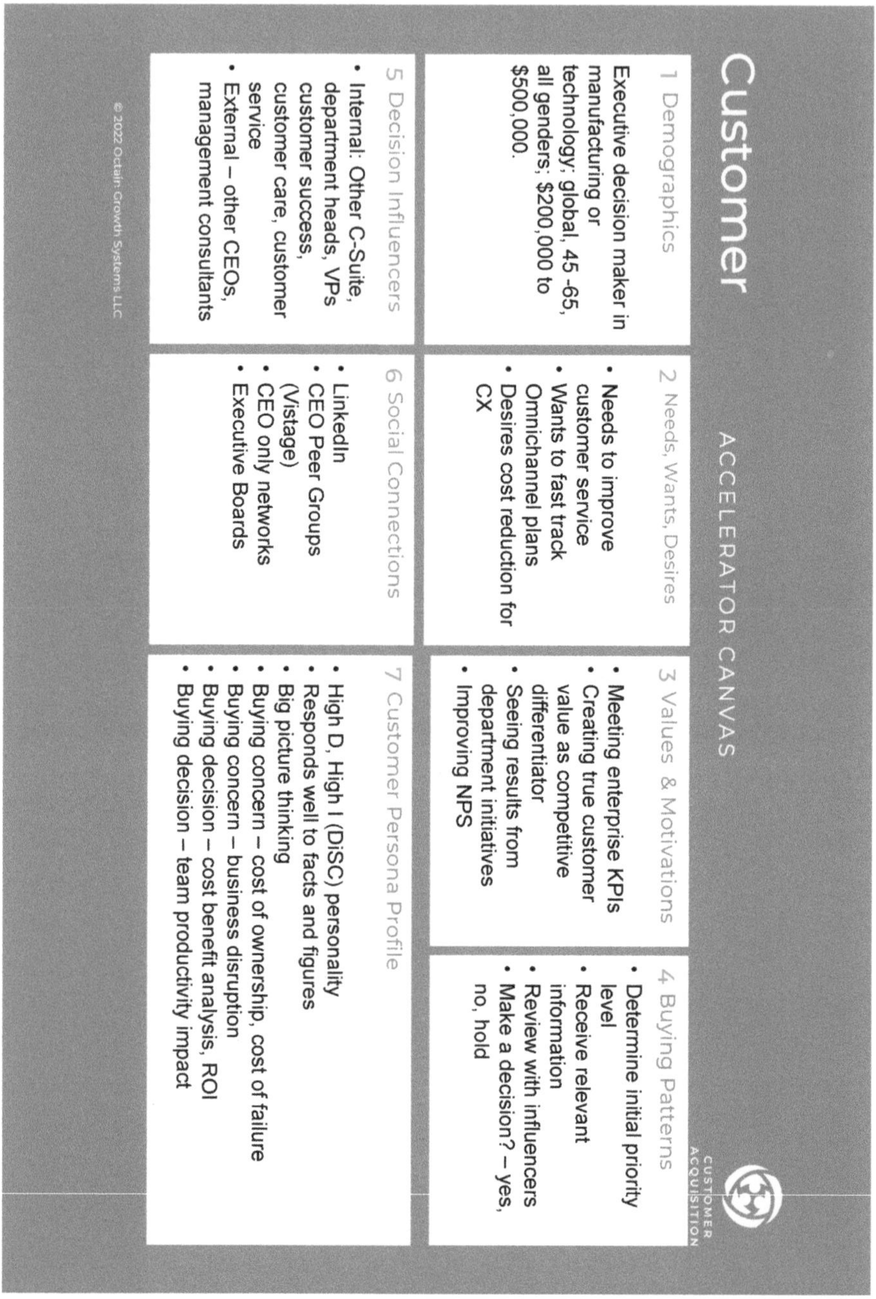
Customer
ACCELERATOR CANVAS
CUSTOMER ACQUISITION
1 Demographics
Executive decision maker in manufacturing or technology; global, 45 -65, all genders; $200,000 to $500,000.
2 Needs, Wants, Desires
• Needs to improve customer service
• Wants to fast track Omnichannel plans
• Desires cost reduction for CX
3 Values & Motivations
• Meeting enterprise KPIs
• Creating true customer value as competitive differentiator
• Seeing results from department initiatives
• Improving NPS
4 Buying Patterns
• Determine initial priority level
• Receive relevant information
• Review with influencers
• Make a decision? – yes, no, hold
5 Decision Influencers
• Internal: Other C-Suite, department heads, VPs customer success, customer care, customer service
• External – other CEOs, management consultants
6 Social Connections
• LinkedIn
• CEO Peer Groups (Vistage)
• CEO only networks
• Executive Boards
7 Customer Persona Profile
• High D, High I (DiSC) personality
• Responds well to facts and figures
• Big picture thinking
• Buying concern – cost of ownership, cost of failure
• Buying concern – business disruption
• Buying decision – cost benefit analysis, ROI
• Buying decision – team productivity impact
© 2022 Octain Growth Systems LLC

Keys To Customer Acceleration

1. Complete a detailed demographic and psychographic profile of your top customer prospects and determine three very specific niche markets.
2. Make a list of your customers' strongest needs, wants, and desires. What problems are they trying to solve? What keeps them awake at night? What drives them crazy?
3. Make a list of your customers' key values and motivations. What do they value most for their business and lives? What are they searching for? What are their strongest needs, desires, and wants?
4. Develop your customers' buying patterns. How do they buy: in store, online, in-person handshake? How often do they need your services: once, occasionally, continually, required, desired, nice to have?
5. Discover influencers. Who most influences or controls their decision to buy?
6. Determine social connections. Where and who do they connect with in social groups, online and off-line: social networks, work, school, community, church?
7. Complete your customer persona. What are the key characteristics of your ideal customer? Consider your best decision-making customers. Describe them in detail. Use the previous canvas section as a guide.

Use the example Customer Accelerator Canvas in the appendix as a guide to summarize all of your ideas, insights, and decisions on the Customer Accelerator Canvas.

You can find more tools and resources for the canvas in the OGS Customer Accelerator Toolbox on our website at www.octaingrowth.com.

Chapter 5
MESSAGE CLARITY

"Nobody knows what we do."

THE FRUSTRATION SHOWED in Greg Dyson's voice and face as we chatted at a local coffee shop. As national sales manager for Sallyport Commercial Finance, he had spent hundreds of hours and thousands of dollars trying to educate customers on the value the company offers in alternative lending solutions. Leads were trickling in. His sales team was making never-ending follow-up calls that rarely yielded a win.

The executive team honestly thought they were telling a great story because it made sense to them. They assumed their customers knew what they meant when they used their financial industry "tribal" language. It's a classic mistake that many business builders make.

People didn't get Sallyport's message because they didn't see how it related to them. Sallyport's communications were a mix of fluffy ad-lite slogans and confusing financial jargon.

Greg engaged Octain to develop a new message and marketing plan. Working with the executive team we developed a messaging plan based on clear, concise, and common language, built on a well-defined set of values. The result? Company growth exploded. Sallyport expanded internationally, establishing three offices in Canada.

Marketing success lives and dies on the message. A message that connects and communicates will convert an interested or skeptical prospect into a lifelong customer. Your message tells the market who you are and what you have to offer. Your message showcases your competitive strength, presence, and market power.

Without a consistent, well-defined message that clearly communicates your company's product and service value to the market, your marketing efforts *will fail.*

A Solid Messaging Plan Makes You More Money

A well-defined messaging plan can cut the time and effort in creating marketing materials, campaigns, and presentations *in half.*

Without a message framework to rely on, your marketing team starts the messaging process all over again each time they begin a new marketing program. This process can take a few hours to days or weeks. This common practice of reinventing the message wheel wastes time and money and creates delays that lose customers.

Say, for example, a three-person marketing team making around $90,000 a year each spends forty hours developing new messaging and marketing plans for a campaign at a team cost of $130/hour, the project cost is $5,200. With a strong messaging plan, the team is more likely to spend about twenty hours, and the program cost drops to $2,600.

The other cost to a lack of a messaging plan is message fragmentation, which will lose you sales. Your messages get fragmented and confusing because they are being pulled in different directions by different people.

Confusing messages confuse customers and prospects, which results in fewer sales and longer sales cycles as salespeople have to clear up the confusion.

Consider the revenue cost of the loss of one customer who chooses a competitor because they have a stronger value/benefit story. Also consider the revenue loss if sales cycles stretch from three months to six months.

Using the Octain Growth System process to develop a clear and consistent message should take your team no more than six to eight hours when working with one of our certified Growth Architects.

It's worth it, isn't it?

Three Keys To A Compelling Message

OGS focuses on the three keys to a compelling message: clarity, consistency, and conversation.

1. *Clarity* means you have a clear focus on what you are saying. You are expressing it in terms your audience can understand. You are not asking them to translate your jargon/expressions into their language. Basically, you make it easy and fast for them to say, "Okay, got it!" Rather than, "Say what?"

2. *Consistency* means you say the same things in the same way often so that your audience knows what to expect from your company, products, and services. That gives them the confidence that when they buy from you they will get what they are expecting. It makes it more likely they will develop a long-term relationship with your company that will lead to repeat business and multiple referrals.

3. *Conversation* means your message to your customers, prospects, and the market is open-ended and engaging with the expectation that your "message" is as much about listening as it is about talking. The days of broadcasting your message with a megaphone and expecting a positive response are long gone. Your message must invite engagement and response. It must be personalized to the specific desires of that particular customer.

Sound like a challenge? It is. But the messaging accelerator canvas can help you create a solid foundation for your messages. This canvas covers the seven components that make up a strong messaging plan.

Messaging Accelerator Canvas

The OGS messaging accelerator canvas contains seven steps, as seen on the next page.

Figure 17: Messaging Accelerator Canvas

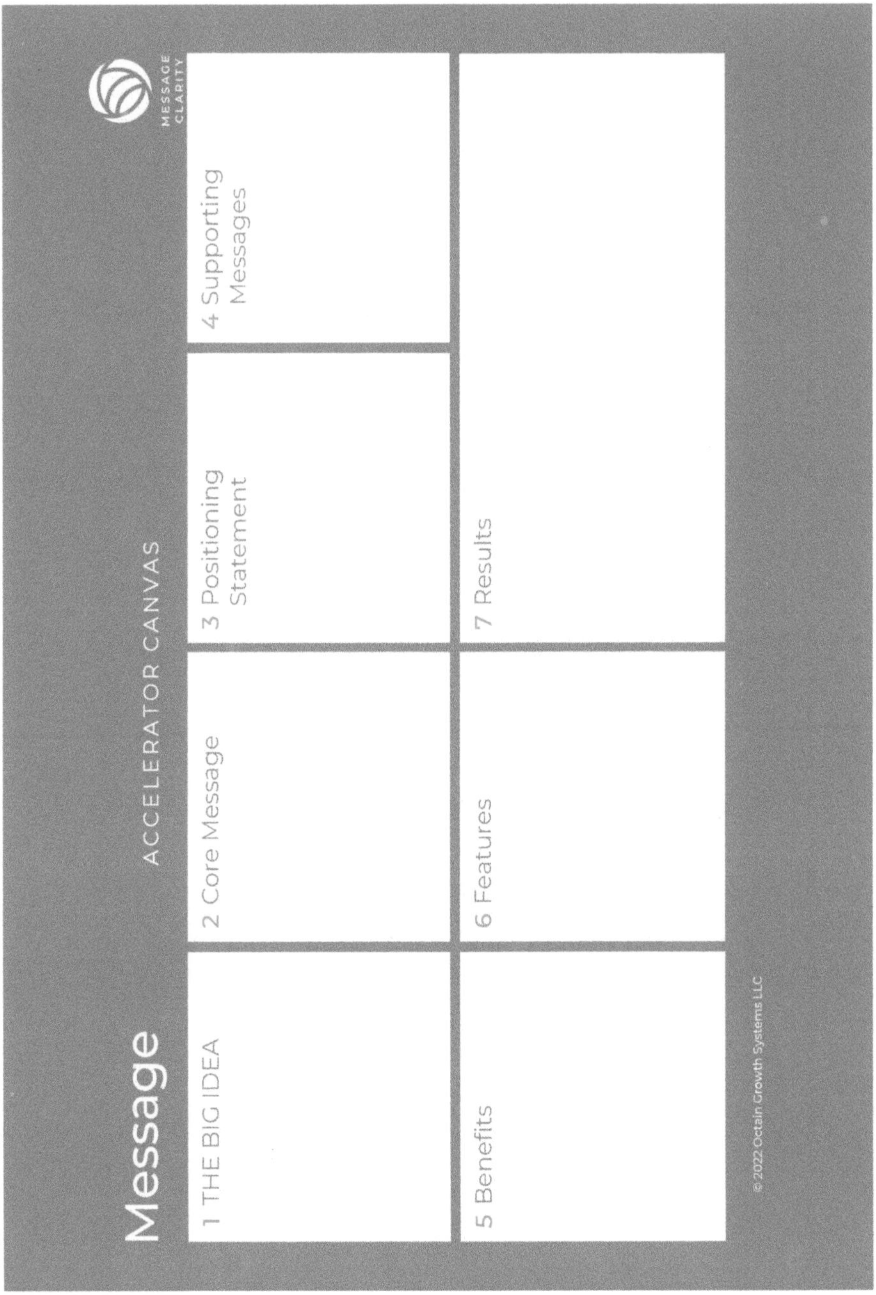
Message
ACCELERATOR CANVAS
MESSAGE CLARITY
1 THE BIG IDEA
2 Core Message
3 Positioning Statement
4 Supporting Messages
5 Benefits
6 Features
7 Results
© 2022 Octain Growth Systems LLC

Seven Steps To Developing A Compelling Message

Figure 18 showcases the process and integration of the seven steps of the messaging accelerator canvas. All are critical to creating an effective message.

Figure 18: Communication Wheel

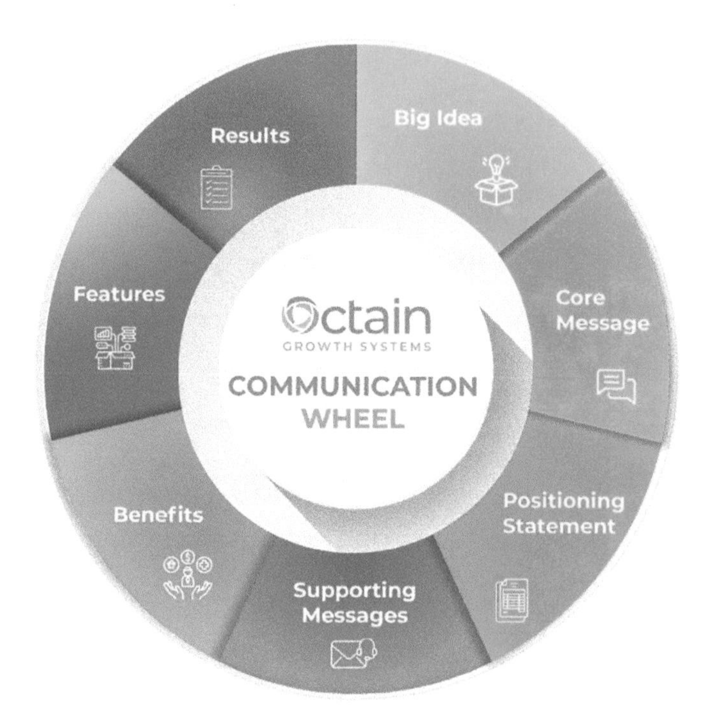

Step 1: The Big Idea

I credit my marketing colleague, Steve Harrison of Bradley Communications,[13] for showing me the critical importance of focusing on the big idea. When you have defined your big idea, the rest of your messaging plan will flow almost effortlessly.

The big idea is *your one thing*. Work with your team to answer the questions in the big idea grid.

Chart 9: Big Idea Grid

The Question	Your Answer
What is the one thing that makes your company and its products or services stand out?	
What captivates your customers and lights up their eyes?	
What creates the passion in your team and employees?	
Express the answers in three to five words and one unique visual.	
Note: The big idea is almost always tied to your vision and mission.	

Your big idea will be a key component of the rest of your messaging plan.

ACTION: Use the big idea grid in Chart 9, above, during creative brainstorming session with your team to draft your big idea.

Step 2: The Core Message

Put simply, this is *why* your company and its products or services exists. It answers the question of why your customers should choose you.

The best and easiest way to define your core message is to use this simple statement, taken from Simon Sinek's great book, *Find Your Why*.[14]

Our company/products/services exists to ____________________ (do what) so that ____________ (our customers will get/feel/experience).

The "do what" is your company's product/service offering.

The "so that" is the impact it has on your customers' businesses and lives.

ACTION: Use the *Find Your Why* statement to draft your core message, which will be used and refined in the positioning statement. Be sure to summarize your work on the canvas.

Step 3: Positioning Statement

The anchor of an effective message plan is a strong positioning statement.

Your positioning statement summarizes your brand values in one clearly expressed statement. It is the statement you use to claim your stake (or territory) in the market. It's a signal to your competitors of where you stand in relationship to them and the rest of the pack.

Start By Knowing Where You Are

Understanding your competitive position and knowing exactly how to position your company, products, and services in the market against others with similar offers will save you thousands of dollars and weeks or months of wasted marketing effort. That's because where you stand in the market—leader, middle of the pack, or follower—determines how you present your products and services to customers and prospects.

Looking for a quick visual way to discover your digital competitive position? Simply search online for your company, products, and services. Whoever comes up ahead of you in the search engine likely comes up ahead of you in your prospect's mind.

Here's a quick look at competitive position and messaging strategies.

Chart 10: Competitive Positioning Strategies

Competitive Position	Strategy
Leader	Emphasize strength and leadership, longevity, the size of the customer base, stay with the leader.
Second or Third Position	Focus on leader's weaknesses with messages that emphasize "Where they are weak, we are strong."
Middle of the Pack	Go where they aren't. Find a new niche for your products. This is often called a Blue Ocean strategy.[15] Rather than competing in the "red ocean" full of sharks, find a "blue ocean" that doesn't yet have access to your product.
Follower	Choose the Blue Ocean strategy referenced above or turn to innovation/new product development to allow you to leapfrog or distance yourself from the competition.

Once you have determined the best positioning strategy, you can develop your positioning statement to emphasize it.

From Struggling Start-up To Consulting Powerhouse

LCS Technologies, an IT consulting firm, was in a very competitive market. As a start-up player in Sacramento, California, LCS focused on helping state and local governments upgrade aging databases. Its competitors were major market leaders like IBM. These large vendors were beating LCS on price because they used less-experienced and less-expensive developers than the LCS team.

LCS needed to position itself so it could compete against these low-priced leaders. To find its competitors' weak spots, we performed a cost-benefit analysis of an LCS solution and an IBM solution based on total project cost, budget, and time to completion. We discovered while the IBM team cost less per developer, their inexperience meant the project took longer and often had errors that had to be corrected, which increased the over all cost of the project.

Armed with this knowledge, LCS positioned itself as the "Elite Technical Team," promoting its team's deep technical experience and expertise. While LCS developers cost more per hour, we proved that the total project cost was lower and fewer mistakes were made during the database transition. The company subsequently was recognized as Sacramento's fastest growing company, with a three-year revenue growth of 2,800 percent.

Developing A Strong Positioning Statement

There are four parts to the positioning statement. Your positioning statement:

1. Defines *who* you are and what you have to offer
2. Answers the key question: *what* is so unique about my company that people will be drawn to our products and services?
3. Defines your approach to the market: *how* your team works with customers and clients
4. Answers *why* your company is the best choice in your industry or service area

Here's how that plays out in practice with a couple of Octain client examples.

Positioning Statement Example #1

Let's unpack the positioning statement for a manufacturing company.

> *Company is the leading supplier of high-quality, thin-gauge thermoformed plastic packaging containers and trays designed and manufactured for excellence. Company's customer-driven,*

innovative design, engineering, and manufacturing teams excel in developing unique, distinctive packaging that has never been done before and takes the customer's concept to the next level of exceptional performance.

Who: Company is the leading supplier of high-quality, thin-gauge thermoformed plastic packaging containers and trays.

What: Products designed and manufactured for excellence.

How: Company's customer-driven, innovative design, engineering, and manufacturing teams.

Why: Excel in developing unique, distinctive packaging that has never been done before.

Positioning Statement Example #2

Let's unpack the positioning statement for a financial services company.

The Financial Company provides financial services that help its clients make effective, strategic decisions through a combination of financial foresight, depth of experience, knowledge, and effective communication of the financial facts. The company acts as an independent counsel and client champion to ensure its clients have the confidence to take the steps they need to achieve their financial goals.

Who: The Financial Company provides financial services that help its clients make effective, strategic decisions.

What: Offers a combination of financial foresight, depth of experience, knowledge, and effective communication of the financial facts.

How: The company acts as an independent counsel and client champion.

Why: To ensure its clients have the confidence to take the steps they need to achieve their financial goals.

ACTION: Draft your own positioning statement in the positioning statement section of the Message Accelerator Canvas in the appendix.

Step 4: Develop Your Supporting Messages

The most common marketing and sales failure point for growing companies is sending out mixed messages. That happens when things are moving fast, and people get out of sync. Supporting messages amplify the big idea, core message, and positioning statement with the most important information you want your customers to know. Supporting messages help you create a clear, compelling, and conversational message your entire team and workforce can share.

Here's a quick and easy process you can use to create supporting messages.

Just answer these four questions:

Figure 19: Supporting Messages Grid

1. Who are you talking to? (Target)
2. How can you help them? (Problem)
3. Why should they care? (Benefit)
4. What happens if they work with you? (Result)

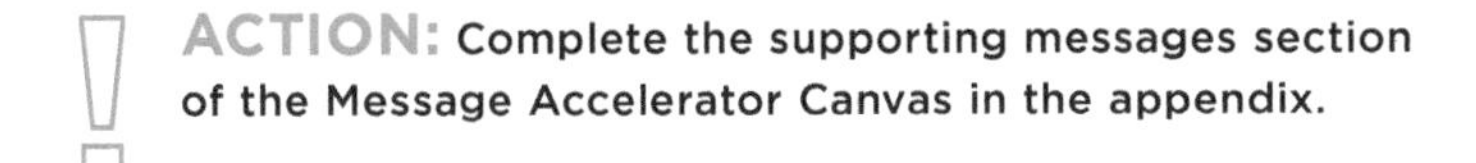

ACTION: Complete the supporting messages section of the Message Accelerator Canvas in the appendix.

Step 5: Create Benefits Statements

In the messaging accelerator canvas, benefit statements expand on supporting messages by adding the next layer of customer connection. Benefit statements clearly communicate the value and reason your customer needs to purchase your products or services. Benefit statements show customers exactly how their lives and businesses will change for the better.

A good benefit statement gets very specific and detailed about the value your company, products, or services delivers to customers.

Here is the process, best done in a team meeting or half-day off-site event:

- Answer the seven value questions below.
- Draft up to twelve benefit statements. (See examples below.)
- Rank the statements based on the marketing and sales strength of the message.
- Choose the top five to seven statements to add to your messaging plan.

Benefit Questions

To create effective benefit statements, answer these seven value questions:

1. How would you describe your business value to me as a brand-new customer?
2. What is the most important thing you offer to your customers?
3. What three words best describe the experience your customers have with your products or services?
4. How do your customers' businesses or lives change when they purchase your products or services?

5. How do these products/services save them time and money?
6. How do these products/services make their life easier and more convenient?
7. What top *two* problems do you solve for your customers when they use your products or services?

Example Benefit Statements

- Company manages client's expectations and mitigates risk so their assets are protected.
- Company's proven system of risk analysis ensures clients are aware of everything happening with the loan and collections.
- Call accounting software from company is the foundation of excellent telecom management and your single source of telecom truth.

ACTION: Schedule a team brainstorming session (preferably off-site) and use the process above to develop your benefit statements.

Step 6: Create Feature Statements

In the messaging accelerator canvas, feature statements expand on supporting messages by giving customers an understanding of how your products/services work.

Feature statements showcase your approach, expand on your competitive advantages, and provide the details of how everything works. Feature statements are your opportunity to show off what your product development team has created. Feature statements are also used to develop competitive market and pricing strategies and protect margins.

The process of developing your feature statements is almost identical to the process to develop benefit statements. The difference is that features emphasize what and how you do what you do.

- Answer the seven value questions below.
- Draft up to twelve benefit statements. (See examples below.)
- Rank the statements based on the marketing and sales strength of the message.
- Choose the top five to seven statements to add to your messaging plan.

Feature Questions

Use these feature questions to highlight what your product/service does for your customers.

1. What is most unique about the way you deliver your products or services?
2. What do your products or services do differently from/better than other competitors in your field or industry?
3. How is the experience of using your products or services different from/better than your competitors?
4. What are the key attributes of your products or services that make them work better than competitive solutions?
5. What do your products/services do that makes your customers' lives easier and more convenient? How does it save them time and money?
6. What five words best describe the results your customers get from your products or services?
7. What are the top three changes or improvements your clients see when they use your products or services?

Example Feature Statements

- Company is agile and flexible, allowing us to be more responsive than other solar integrators. Clients deal directly with a project team that never hesitates. We will always solve the problem, exactly when you need it solved.
- Company understands the packaging needs of specialty bakery, deli, and artisan food producers so well they can recommend packaging options that will provide you with the highest cost/value solution.

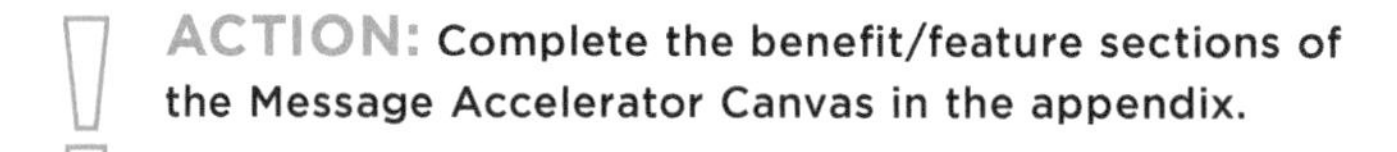

ACTION: Complete the benefit/feature sections of the Message Accelerator Canvas in the appendix.

Step 7: Showcase Your Results

It's time to summarize the positioning and messaging work you have done using the messaging accelerator canvas. You will use it as the message foundation for all your marketing and sales programs and through all your communication channels and opportunities.

Here are just a few ways to start using your messaging plan.

- To create your elevator pitch.
- To create an outline for your speaking engagements.
- To create the text for all your marketing materials: your brochure copy, postcards, letters, emails, newsletters, and website. Use the phrases in these statements as key points for your copy to make sure you are talking about the *value* you offer, not just the features (things you do).
- To ensure consistency. *Everything* you write or say should be checked against these statements to ensure clarity and consistency in what you communicate about your company, products, or services. It's called staying on message and it dramatically increases your ability to communicate effectively.
- To create memorable connections. Phrases and themes that are consistently and clearly repeated stick with us. How many jingles and songs do you remember because you heard them over and over again? You want your key themes to be memorable to your audience as well. Repeat them.

Figure 20: Example Messaging Accelerator Canvas

Once completed your Message Accelerator Canvas may look something like this.

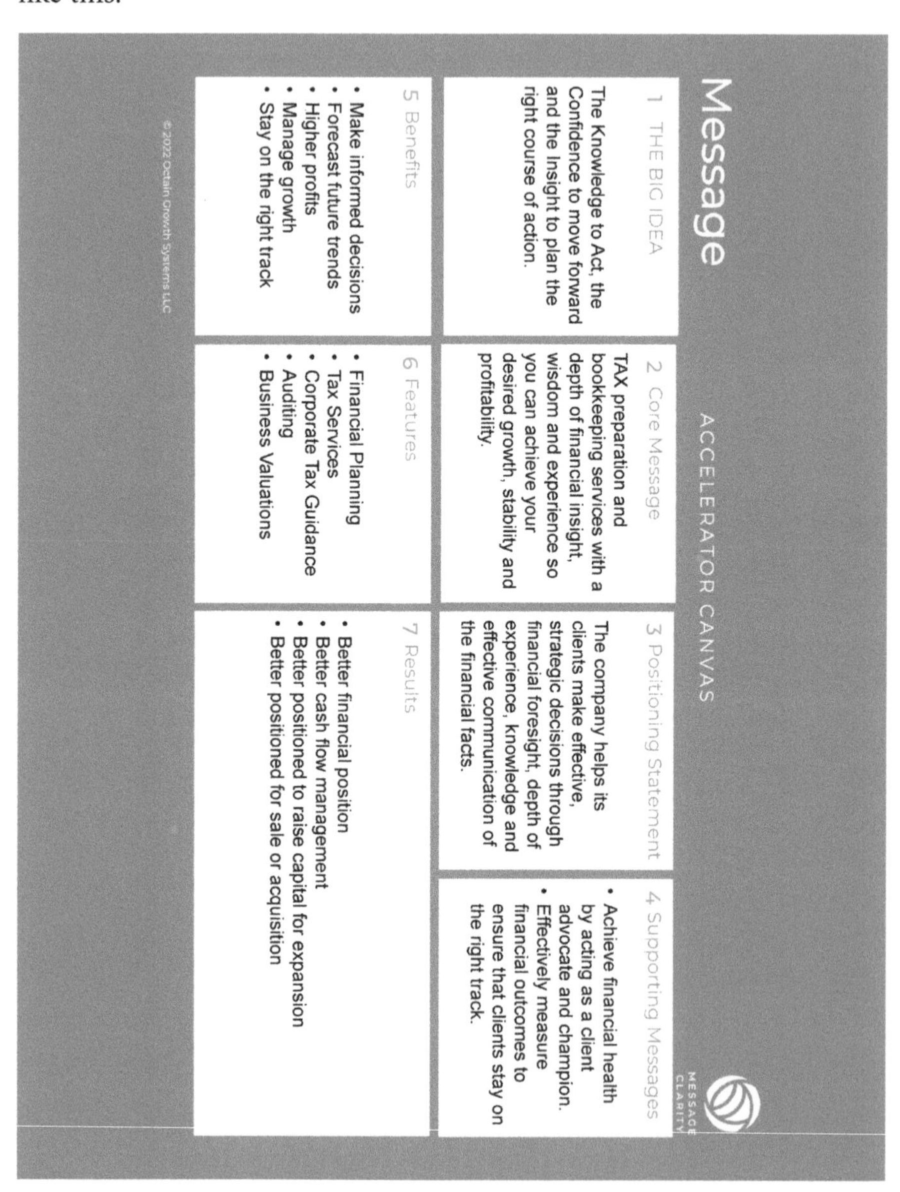

Keys To Message Acceleration

Your messaging plan will pay off in time, money, and energy saved. It gives execution power to all of your marketing programs:

- The big idea—Your *what*. What is the one thing you offer/do that captivates your customers and lights up their eyes with excitement?
- Core message—Your *why*. Why your company and its products or services exist and why your customers should choose you.
- Positioning statement—Your *how*. Describes who you are in your market space, the unique value you bring to your customers, and how you bring it into the market. This is how your big idea gets into the hands of your customers.
- Supporting messages—Your *what*, *why*, and *how* amplified. These are three to five statements that capture your brand value and key benefits.
- Benefits—Their *why*. Benefits are all about your customer. What changes occur in your customer's business or life from your product or service?
- Features—Their *what*. Features are all about how what you do equips and/or provides for your customers.
- Your results—List how you will use your messaging plan through your marketing and sales communications and distribution channels.

ACTION: Use the example Message Accelerator Canvas in the appendix as a guide to summarize all of your ideas, insights, and decisions on the Message Accelerator Canvas.

You can find more tools and resources for the canvas in the OGS Message Accelerator Toolbox on our website at www.octaingrowth.com.

Chapter 6
MARKET EXPANSION

Good marketing makes the company look smart.
Great marketing makes the customer feel smart.—
Joe Chernov, Chief Marketing Officer, Pendo

American River Tax Services (ARTS) had a thriving tax services practice in Sacramento. That was the problem. Although ARTS has the capacity to provide extensive bookkeeping services and tax planning, those services and employees were vastly underutilized. It also left the company with revenue gaps during non-tax season months.

ARTS engaged Octain to develop a new marketing strategy. We created customer canvases for three target market segments: tax preparation, tax planning and bookkeeping. We then created a marketing strategy based around a brand and market awareness campaign that included social media, social advertising and direct mail.

As a result, ARTS revenues increased 35 percent within the first twelve months of launching their new marketing campaign.

Redefine Your Marketing Engine

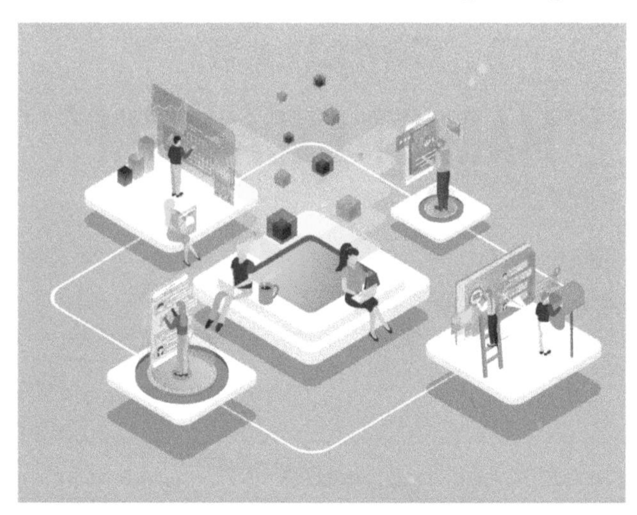

This is the fun part. It's where all the work you've done in the brand, messaging, and customer accelerator canvases pays off. Think of these as the pistons that create the force that accelerates your marketing efforts.

It's your marketing and sales engine that delivers company revenue growth and profitability. It's your marketing engine that opens up new markets and customers for your goods and services and gives you the edge over your competitors.

As a marketer, you know the role of marketing has been misunderstood—*for too long, by too many business owners and management consultants*. It has been considered an expense, a cost center, and for some a necessary evil to reaching business goals.

I think that has been the case because traditional marketing is very expensive and nearly impossible to measure. Revenues increase, but how much of that is due to marketing efforts?

As department store magnate John Wanamaker famously complained:

> *"Half the money I spend on advertising is wasted; the trouble is, I don't know which half."*[16]

It's different today. With today's digital marketing, you can track and measure the impact. You can see day by day, hour by hour, how well your marketing efforts are working. You can and should connect marketing spend to revenue increases. Today's marketers need to know their numbers as well as the company CFO does.

Marketing should be profitable, states the Content Marketing Institute (CMI), and here is its long-held definition of content marketing: "*A strategic marketing approach of creating and distributing valuable, relevant, and consistent content to attract and acquire a clearly defined audience—with the objective of driving profitable customer action.*"[17]

My colleague Dennis Shiao takes it one step further. This definition is especially true for start-up, non-profit, and benefit organizations: "*A strategic marketing approach of creating and distributing valuable, relevant, and consistent content to attract and acquire a clearly defined audience—with the objective of driving meaningful action.*"[18]

Here's the bottom line: if you want to accelerate business growth, it's time to move marketing out of the cost center and into the *profit* center. It's time to acknowledge the *impact* marketing can have on your business operations when it is well executed.

And smart execution of marketing is what the OGS is all about.

Focus Your Efforts

As a function, modern marketing is huge. And of course we can't cover it all. We wouldn't even begin to try.

Instead, we will focus on what we have found to be the most successful strategies and tactics used for modern marketing in this digital-first, remote-work world: to develop and implement an integrated marketing plan. The difference with OGS is *integrated.*

Too often, business builders develop revenue-producing strategies and plans in silos. The communications team sets the message, marketing creates its plans, and sales takes another direction. Within OGS, all six accelerators are connected. As you move through the marketing canvas, you will see how the branding, customer, and messaging work previously completed gets brought in.

It is that cumulative integration of accelerators that delivers real business growth.

Joe Zaniker of ThirdRail brought Octain into California Laboratory Services (CLS) in 2019. Joe's team was developing a new brand image and needed an integrated messaging and marketing strategy to increase brand awareness and market presence. As a specialty business in the very specific niche of environmental chemistry testing, CLS didn't need the typical broad demand and lead generation strategies most marketers would automatically employ. The company needed to reach a well-defined set of prospective customers and be seen as the top expert in the field by other scientists and well as the CEOs.

The challenge was that most of the initial buyer's journey was done by the CEO's administrative assistant or program coordinator, while the buying decision was made by the CEO or scientist. These were very different customers with different values, motivations, and buying patterns all part of the same buyer's journey.

The company's integrated marketing plan focused on thought leadership with website content, blogs to showcase the company's scientific expertise, account-based marketing with a tiger-team sales effort to laser focus on key accounts, and an aggressive search engine optimization (SEO) effort for that initial research step by the administrative assistant.

Customizing the integrated marketing plan to CLS's unique set of circumstances helped them land several large industrial customers within a few months of launching the plan.

The market accelerator canvas below was used to achieve that success. This accelerator canvas is designed to help you create an integrated marketing strategy that is unique to your company's marketing needs. It works with the smart execution process to provide the highest ROI for you.

Figure 21: Octain Market Accelerator Canvas

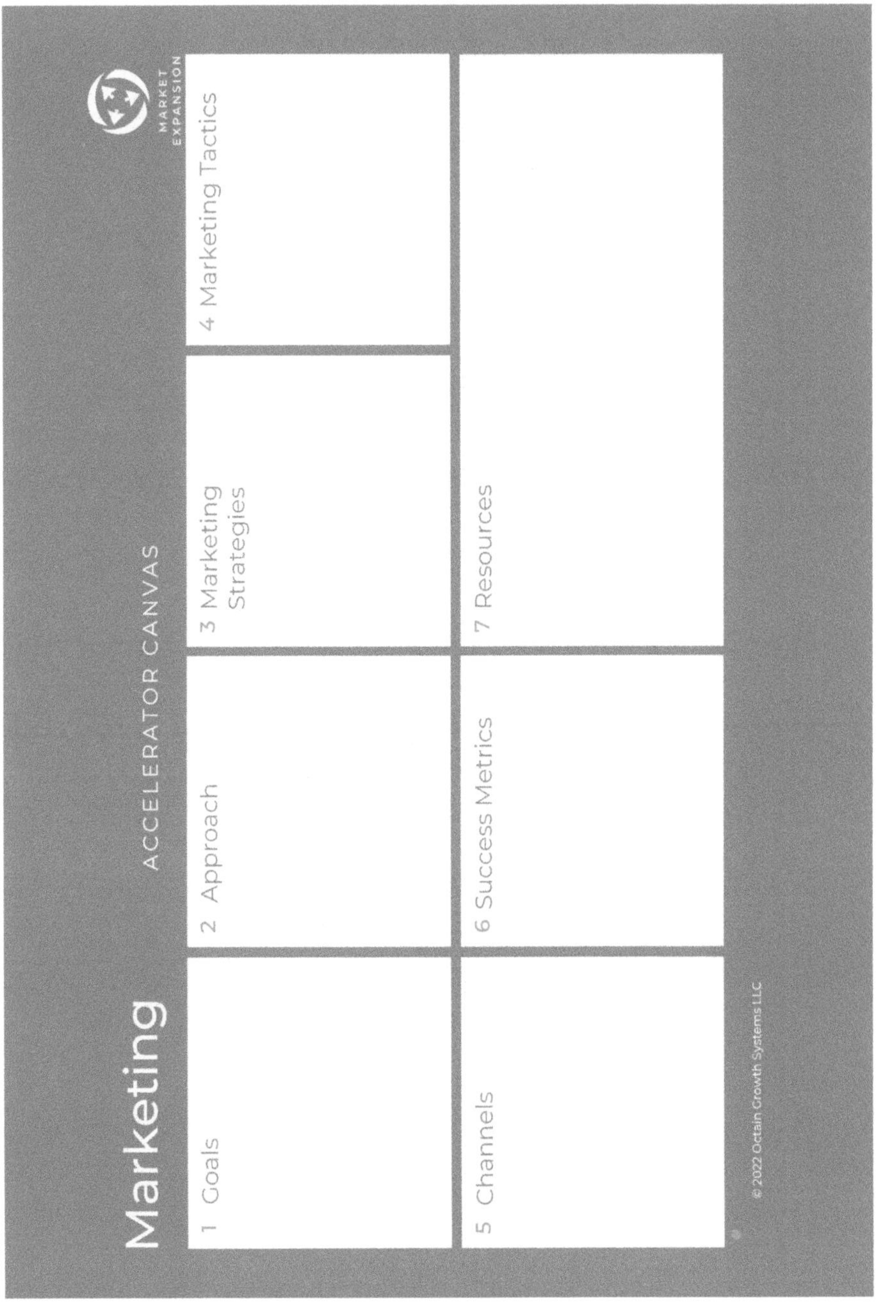
Marketing
ACCELERATOR CANVAS
MARKET EXPANSION
1 Goals
2 Approach
3 Marketing Strategies
4 Marketing Tactics
5 Channels
6 Success Metrics
7 Resources
© 2022 Octain Growth Systems LLC

Here are the seven steps of the Octain Marketing Accelerator Canvas:

1. Goals—Desired market/customer increase in revenue, volume, and numbers.
2. Approach—Where will you focus your marketing strategies and activities?
3. Marketing strategies—Your game plan for reaching your goals.
4. Marketing tactics—The actions you will take to reach your goals.
5. Channels—How you will distribute your goods and services to your customers.
6. Success metrics—How will you measure ROI?
7. Resources—The time, money, energy, talent, and tools you need to meet your target market goals.

Step 1: Determine Your Business Goals

Goals. Love them or hate them. We know we need them. I'm reminded of the well-known Zig Ziglar quote: *"If you aim at nothing, you will hit it every time."*

Here are the business goal types to consider in reaching your desired market/customer increase in revenue, volume, and numbers.

- Revenue and profitability goals. How much do you want to make next year?
- Brand goals. How can you expand your company's market presence?
- Customer goals. What kind of customer growth would you like to see?
- Marketing and sales goals. What ROI are you looking to achieve from your marketing efforts?

- Employee, partner, and vendor goals. How can you best support the success of your employees, partners, and vendors?
- For each goal type, include the following:
- Desired outcome. This is where you want to be when you reach your goal.
- Specific result. This is a quantitative number or percentage that can be measured.
- Time-frame. When do you expect to achieve this goal? This can be set in terms of months, end points, dates, etc.
- Milestones. What steps will you take to reach this goal? Recording milestones helps you chart your progress.

This is an example of business goals for an HVAC repair service company.

Chart 11: Business Goals For A Repair Service Company

GOAL TYPE	DESIRED OUTCOME	SPECIFIC RESULT (NUMBER)	TIME-FRAME	MILESTONES
Revenue	Increase revenues	By 20 percent	Year-end 2021	5 percent per quarter for 2021
Brand	Shift from residential to commercial business image	Redesign website to be 50 percent more commercial products	September 2021	Hire web developer in April New content and photos by June Completed site by September
Marketing	Increase maintenance customers	From 50 to 100 customers	September 2021	10 percent by March 20 percent by June 20 percent by September
Sales/ Customer	Increase commercial customers	From 46 to 70	Year-end 2021	2 new customers per month
Employee	Hire new service techs	Three	One each quarter until September	Ad out in March First hire June Second hire July Third hire September

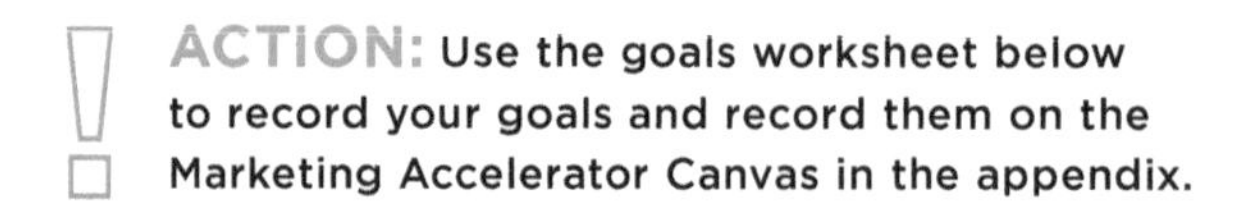
ACTION: Use the goals worksheet below to record your goals and record them on the Marketing Accelerator Canvas in the appendix.

Chart 12: Goals Worksheet

GOAL TYPE	DESCRIPTION	DESIRED OUTCOME	SPECIFIC RESULT (NUMBER)	TIME-FRAME	MILESTONES

Step 2: Approach

There are hundreds of ways to approach marketing. The number of options available is one of the most confusing, time-consuming, and money wasting challenges you have when choosing how to market your products and services.

OGS focuses on the four common marketing approaches that deliver growth. Virtually all strategies and tactics can be aligned with one or more of these approaches as outlined in chart 13 on the next page.

Chart 13: Major Marketing Approaches

APPROACH	DEFINITION	EXAMPLES	BEST FOR
INBOUND	Bringing customers to you first by attracting their attention and providing resources and content they need before you try to sell them something. Focused on building relationships before selling.	Content marketing, blogging, SEO, and opt-in email marketing	Lead generation
OUTBOUND	The process of promoting a product through continued outreach via sales and marketing channels to customers who may or may not know you or want your products and services.	Advertising, radio, TV, promotions, direct mail, digital ads, public relations, and outbound sales	Demand generation
LEAD GENERATION	The action or process of identifying and cultivating potential customers for a business' products or services.	Content marketing, website, blogging, SEO, opt-in email marketing, webinars, and sales presentations	Identifying and closing prospects
DEMAND GENERATION	The action or process of creating interest in your product and services across a wide range of customers and markets.	Trade shows, content marketing, advertising, social media, and brand promotion	Attracting a large pool of potential prospects

For many business builder clients, focusing on inbound marketing to deliver lead generation provides the best ROI. For established expanding businesses, a mix of fifty/fifty, inbound to outbound/demand generation, is most effective.

ACTION: Complete the marketing approach section of the Marketing Accelerator Canvas in the appendix.

Step 3: Marketing Strategies

Affordable Furniture & Blinds, a boutique furniture store in Placerville, California, was struggling to compete against the big furniture chain stores in affluent El Dorado County. Every day, a salesperson would pitch the two owners, Pete and Jill Bennet, on a new marketing or advertising program that was getting great results for other clients. But, as the disclaimer goes for weight loss programs, "results not typical."

The Bennets tried many of the marketing and advertising tactics, including newspaper and radio advertising, and digital yellow pages. The campaigns were expensive. The results were disappointing.

The Bennets were experiencing the number one failure point of marketing: the lack of an integrated marketing plan. After they developed one, revenues increased 10 percent in the next twelve months. The Bennets spent less time on marketing and more time with customers, and the best part, according to Jill, was when the pesky salespeople showed up, she would simply say, "it's not in my plan" and go on with her day.

Without an integrated marketing plan, marketing is scattershot, trial and error, "spray and pray." And the result is painful on so many levels:

- Money and time are wasted
- Revenues decrease, profits decline
- Marketing takes a hit by losing budget, people may be fired, and careers are sidelined.

Developing Your Marketing Strategy

OGS starts the process with discovery, followed by evaluation, and then choosing an optimum marketing mix based on the strongest forecasted ROI.

This process is called *smart execution*:

- *Discover.* Explore your options. There are 1,001 things you can do to market your business. You should only do a few of them. Which ones are right for you? That's what you discover when you explore your options.

- *Evaluate current strengths.* There's no need to reinvent the wheel; it's better to build on success. By understanding your current situation, you can choose additional strategies and actions that increase the power of your marketing programs.
- *Move forward.* Choosing the optimum marketing mix is the combination of factors such as pricing, channels, and sales and marketing activities used to enhance customer purchasing decisions.

Explore Your Options

Here are the strategies that comprise an integrated marketing plan. Different marketing plans are needed for different reasons at different times.

Chart 14: Marketing Strategy Options

MARKETING STRATEGY	DEFINITION	WHY USE	WHEN TO USE
Advertising	The activity or profession of producing advertisements for commercial products or services.	For widespread product/service promotion.	Product launches, sales and events, special offers.
Channel	Means of distribution of goods and services.	For indirect product/service sales through a dealer, distributor, vendor, partner, or affiliate marketer; to cover a wider geographic area.	Opening a new market, promoting wider distribution, building your brand in niche markets, increasing sales of a less popular product, shifting the sales burden to a third party.

Community	Engaged customers sometimes called tribes that actively promote your products and services to their connections without compensation.	Connect existing customers with prospects globally, connect prospects with each other globally, increase customers, get instant customer feedback, and enable product testing and market research.	Your digital communities will be the primary place to build deep customer relationships, loyal customers, and identify new customer needs.
Influencer	Bloggers, celebrities, and big-name customers with large audiences who actively promote your products and services to their connections, often with compensation.	Develop brand awareness, demand generation, market expansion.	Product promotion, brand building, market expansion.
Content	Marketing that involves the creation and sharing of material (such as videos, blogs, articles, and social media posts) that does not explicitly promote a brand but is intended to stimulate interest in its products or services.	Connect and engage with prospects to build customer relationships.	Lead generation, thought leadership, product/service education, support event marketing.

Direct Mail	Printed and mailed advertising pieces like letters, postcards, promotional gifts, catalogs.	Reach large groups of prospects, often in a specific geographic area.	Great for brick-and-mortar businesses and storefronts.
Email	Digital equivalent of direct mail.	Nurture prospects not yet ready to buy; reach specific audiences with targeted offers; inform, educate, stay connected, build relationships.	Share news and information, nurture prospects, stay top-of-mind with customers.
Events	The process of developing a themed exhibit, display, or presentation to promote a product, service, cause, or organization leveraging in-person (or digital) engagement.	Product showcase; competitive positioning, relationship building, and networking.	Product launches and sales pushes; brand, market, and industry exposure; lead generation.
SEO	The process of improving the quality and quantity of website traffic to a website or a web page from search engines.	Get found in search engines, the first place most people go to begin their buying journey.	When you actively use your website for marketing; expert SEO can be expensive—basic meta tagging is the minimum for some SEO.

SEM (Search Marketing)	The process of gaining traffic and visibility from search engines through paid and unpaid efforts. Paid is usually called pay per click (PPC).	Gain better control over how and when your company is found in search engines.	To increase brand, product, and company visibility on the internet.
Social Media	The use of social media platforms to connect with your audience to build your brand, increase sales, and drive website traffic.	Increase brand awareness and lead generation; educate, inform, and grow your audiences.	Drive traffic to your website, brand building, amplify your message, increase audience size, list building.

Evaluate Your Strengths

Consider all the marketing strategies in the integrated marketing plan, and have your team evaluate the performance and costs of each one: Was it high performing or low performing? How much money was spent? How much time did it take to complete?

Using these performance and costs metrics to determine the ROI of that strategy to see where it should fit in your overall marketing mix.

Chart 15: Evaluate Your Current Marketing Strengths

MARKETING STRATEGY	PERFORMANCE METRIC (Rank from 1 [low] to 10 [high])	MONEY SPENT (Total dollars spent on this program)	PEOPLE AND TIME USED (Total number of person-hours expended on this program)	RESULTS (ROI)
Advertising				
Channel				
Community				
Influencer				
Content				
Direct Mail				
Email				
Events				
SEO				
SEM (PPC)				
Social Media				

Move Forward, Choosing Your Marketing Mix

Your marketing mix is the set of strategies that when combined in your integrated marketing plan will offer you the highest level of revenue growth with the best ROI. A classic marketing mix looks at the promotion, price, product, and place, as noted in Figure 22.

Figure 22: Example Marketing Mix

Based on the success quotients highlighted in your marketing strength evaluation and your business goals, choose the top three to five strategies to be included in your integrated marketing plan.

You can do more than five, but our work has shown that three to five strategies is optimal for most small to medium-size business marketing departments on a quarter-by-quarter basis due to the resources required for implementation.

ACTION: Use chart 16 below to determine your marketing strategies based on your current strengths from chart 15 and desired marketing mix in figure 22. Summarize the results on the Marketing Accelerator Canvas in the appendix.

Chart 16: Choose Your Marketing Strategies

MARKETING STRATEGY	PRIORITY (Rank from 1 [low] to 10 [high])	MARKETING SPEND (Total dollars to be spent on this program)	PEOPLE AND TIME NEEDED (Total number of people and time resources required)	METRICS/ KPIs (Projected ROI)
Advertising				
Channel				
Community				
Influencer				
Content				
Direct Mail				
Email				
Events				
SEO				
SEM (PPC)				
Social Media				

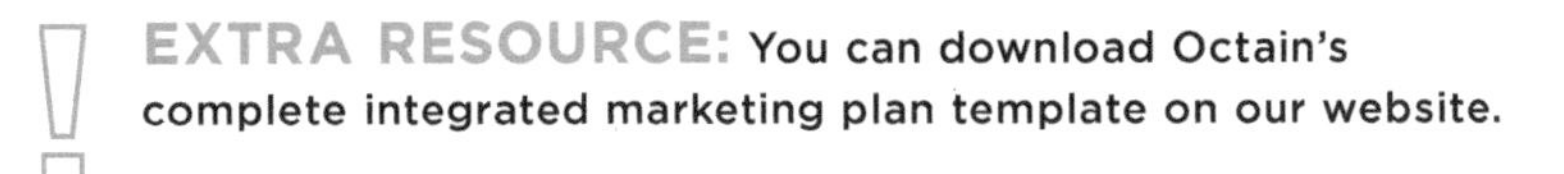

EXTRA RESOURCE: You can download Octain's complete integrated marketing plan template on our website.

Step 4: Marketing Tactics

Marketing tactics include everything you do to bring attention to your company, products, and services to create market demand, obtain customers and sales, and grow revenue.

Top Performing Marketing Tactics

Marketing tactics fall into the following categories:

- *Collateral.* Marketing collateral is physical and digital. Physical marketing materials include items like business cards, postcards, brochures, direct mail, coupons, and newspaper ads. Digital collateral is the digital equivalent of those items. Any marketing piece sent physically or electronically or physically handed out is considered collateral.
- *Content.* Over the last fifteen years, content marketing has become the most popular form of marketing because it is one of the most effective. Content marketing involves the creation and sharing of material (such as videos, blogs, articles, and social media posts) that does not explicitly promote a brand but is intended to engage interest, entertain, and inform the audience.
- *Campaigns.* Campaigns are active promotions created as a series of actions. The method may vary from direct mail, internet ads, social media, etc. What makes it a campaign is that the activity is done multiple times over a set time period.
- *Advertising.* Referred to as a subset of marketing or sometimes as its own discipline or niche, advertising is a direct promotion with a specific offer to buy, make a buying decision, or take immediate action. What differentiates

advertising from other forms of marketing is the requirement for action and the inclusion of a specific offer.

- *Digital marketing.* Any marketing activity that takes place on or through the internet. This includes websites, digital ads, email, mobile/wireless marketing, digital consumer data including analytics (like Google Analytics and Facebook Insights) as well as electronic customer relationship marketing (eCRM). Digital marketing is unique in that it combines the creative and technical (IT) aspects of marketing.
- *Events.* Events include trade shows, conferences, meetings, meetups, and networking opportunities. Event marketing is the process of developing a themed exhibit, display, or presentation to promote a product, service, cause, or organization leveraging in-person (or now digital) engagement.
- *Social media marketing.* Any marketing activity that is directed to or from a social sharing site or community is considered social media marketing. All social media marketing is also digital marketing, but all digital marketing is not social media marketing.

Marketing Objectives

Tactics are effective only when they are linked to objectives. Here we examine the five types of marketing objectives you will use in your marketing plan: continuous market presence, brand building, lead generation, customer relationship building and industry impact. Each of your tactics should fulfill one or more of these objectives.

The primary marketing objectives are illustrated in figure 23.

Figure 23: Marketing Objectives

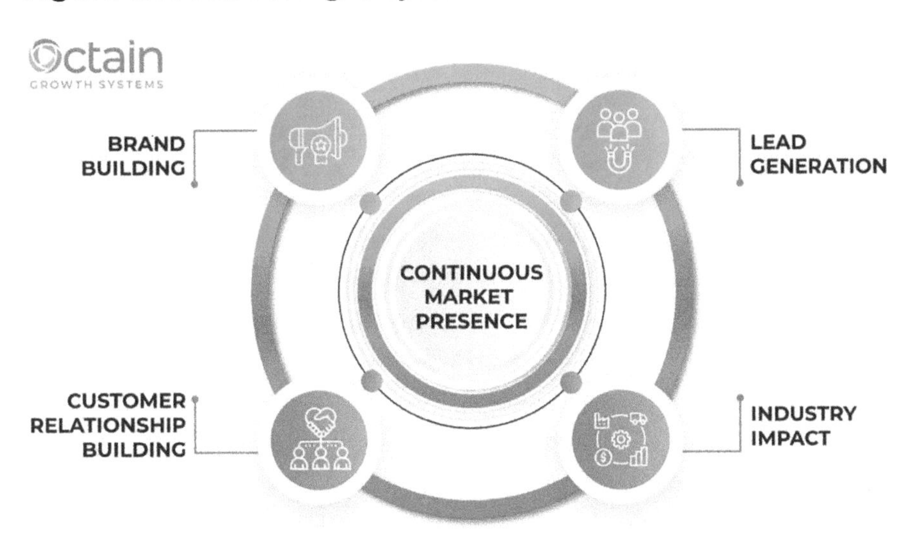

Continuous Market Presence

These are marketing activities done on a regular, consistent basis in the same format or publication and/or to the same target audience. The objective is to keep your brand and services in front of your prospects and customers with frequent, ongoing exposure. Examples are regular advertising in key publications; websites; regular, scheduled direct mailings, e-zines, or newsletters; public relations; and internet marketing programs.

Brand Building

These activities are directed toward building your brand in the general market. These are the image activities that make people aware of your services, your brand, new programs, etc. Regular image-building activities are a key part of any branding campaign.

Lead Generation

These are marketing activities targeted at generating leads and attracting more prospects. While all marketing activities should be aimed at generating leads, the programs and activities referred to here are solely designed to generate leads. Examples are telemarketing, text marketing, direct and email promotions, trade shows, point of sale displays in stores, affiliate partnerships, and online marketing campaigns.

Customer Relationship Building

These activities focus on contacts made through personal interaction, including clubs; professional groups and organizations; and school, church, and social activities. This also includes past and present clients and your referral network or system. An important and underutilized activity here is a customer council, a board of customers who can help you develop effective customer experience strategies.

Industry Impact

These activities are designed to increase your competitive presence in your industry or market space. They emphasize industry influence and thought leadership. Examples of industry impact activities are events, tradeshows, hosted conferences and/or major sponsorships like a charity or community event.

Putting It All Together

These marketing objectives create both the reason and the results of your activity. Your integrated marketing strategy should have campaigns, activities, and tactics that meet each of these objectives so it is balanced across the key revenue-producing accelerators.

A common mistake is focusing on one objective like lead generation without understanding that it requires elements of the other four to be effective. That's why it's called an *integrated* marketing plan.

Running An Effective Campaign

Campaigns are the lifeblood of effective, integrated marketing using OGS. To understand how to run an effective campaign, it's helpful to understand how your customer responds to a marketing campaign.

Customer Response Cycle

The Customer Response Cycle includes the five Rs (recognition, recall, reach, reward, response); one A (awareness); and a P (permission).

Figure 24 illustrates how these seven factors work together.

Figure 24: Customer Response Cycle

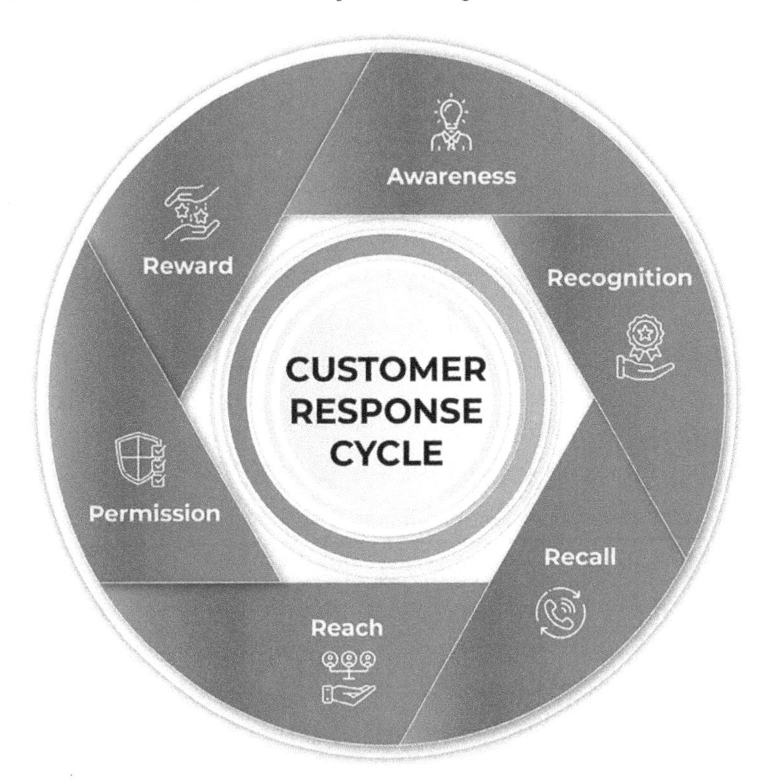

From the customers' point of view, they are defined as follows:

- *Awareness*—I know you are out there. You are on my radar screen.
- *Recognition*—I recognize you when I see you. I know what you do/offer.

- *Recall*—I remember who you are. I think of your company, product, or service without a specific memory jog or reminder. Or I know more about your company than just the name or logo. I remember a value or benefit you have stated.
- *Reach*—I am interested in what you have to offer. I am not ready to buy but I am seeking more information, so I am reaching for you. I may check products on your website and/or read customer reviews of your services. I may check in with friends to get their opinion of your company. I may sign up for your newsletter.
- *Permission*—Because I have reached out for you and if I have given you my contact information, I have given you permission to contact me, engage me in conversation, and give me a reason to take the next step to do business with you.
- *Reward*—I need an incentive to do business with you. If the prospective customer has asked a question directly or opted in for your newsletter or blog, it's time to reward them with something that lets them "try out" your product or service—a free level of usage or a free trial period are almost required today, as is a coupon if appropriate.
- *Response*—I will respond to your reward with my next move. That next move can be to stay connected but take no action, take action and engage to purchase, say no because this is not for me, or say not now and disengage because the product or service is not the right fit now. I might be back.

You can see how the customers' relationship with and engagement with you shifts over time as they get to know you and your company better. That is the purpose of an effective campaign.

ACTION: Complete the marketing tactics section of the Marketing Accelerator Canvas in the appendix.

Step 5: Channels

With OGS, the first step is always discovery. When it comes to channels, that means looking beyond the tried-and-true ways you are comfortable distributing your products and finding new ways to reach current and new customers.

In 2020, when the COVID-19 lockdowns happened, stores closed and shifted to online sales. Salespeople who were used to traveling to customers had to learn to sell through Zoom or Microsoft Teams. Even as we return to more normal buying patterns, the lesson for marketers is to discover new channels of distribution. The reward is market expansion and acceleration.

When it comes to channels, your choices break down into these primary categories:

- direct and indirect
- digital and traditional
- paid, earned, and owned media—channels that apply most specifically to content marketing and refer to ways to get your content in front of your audience

Chart 17 summarizes the considerations of what, when, and how to use these channel options.

Chart 17: Choosing The Best Channels

MARKETING STRATEGY	DEFINITION	WHY TO USE	WHEN TO USE
Direct	Can be in-person or digital.	Establish personal relationships; understand customer needs, wants, and desires without a third-party filter; anticipate customer behavior.	New business, new market; product launches, special sales, and offers; digital subscriptions; complex and high value/luxury sales.
Indirect	Through a third party.	Expand distribution capacity, scale growth for low-cost, high-volume products.	Faster expansion, wider distribution, product requires specialty knowledge of market or product.
Digital	Can be broadly broken into seven main categories: SEO, SEM, PPC, social media, content, email, and mobile marketing.	Lower cost of distribution, 24/7 operation, engaging and interactive capabilities, most customers' preferred way of shopping today.	Reach more customers and markets, lower cost of distribution and operations, improve customer engagement.
Traditional	Any type of marketing that is off-line, not digital.	Reach local community, expand brand awareness, promote stability and brand strength, longevity of materials, and message control.	Specific audience reach, e.g., TV station; niche marketing, i.e., by zip code; mass communication.

Paid Media	External marketing efforts that involve a paid placement, such as pay-per-click advertising, branded content, and display ads.	Increase search engine traffic, lead generation, and promote content.	Lead generation, increase web traffic, and promote sales and special offers.
Earned Media	Media exposure you've earned through word-of-mouth.	Increase brand strength and recognition, thought leadership, and audience authority.	Create earned media opportunities through an effective content and social media program.
Owned Media	Content you control, e.g., your company website, blog, and social media accounts.	Lead generation and nurturing, expand audience reach and thought leadership.	As your primary content marketing program and channel.

ACTION: Complete the distribution channels section of the Marketing Accelerator Canvas in the appendix by listing your preferred channels on your canvas.

Step 6: Success Metrics

If marketing is to shift from a cost center to a profit center, it must be centered on ROI. When you can show the revenue results of your labors, you will receive more budget dollars, leadership recognition, and more opportunities for career advancement.

Tracking the results of your marketing campaigns is easier than ever. Even traditional marketing efforts can be tracked more effectively as they are often attached to a landing page, website, or social media account.

Here are the key marketing success factors we have found most valuable in our work with clients:

- marketing revenue attribution
- customer acquisition cost
- customer churn ratios
- customer lifetime value (LTV)
- digital marketing ROI
- brand mentions
- traffic-to-lead ratio (new contact rate)
- lead-to-customer ratio (conversions)
- landing page conversion rates
- social media traffic (and conversion rates)
- mobile traffic, leads, and conversion rates
- overall impressions
- cost-per-lead
- cost-per-sale
- return on engagement (ROE)
- Net Promoter Score (NPS) measures the loyalty of the customers to a company.

To get a true picture of marketing performance, success metrics should include multichannel data collection and off-line data integration. It should provide a whole picture of past performance and allow for predictive behavior analysis, modeling, and forecasting.

ACTION: List your preferred tracking metrics from the above list on your canvas.

Step 7: Resources

When most entrepreneurs and business builders think of resources, the top two that always spring to mind are time and money. Time and money are often the critical gatekeepers that can make or break success in all your business operations, not just marketing. However, time and money are just two of the resources a company needs to be successful. The other three are energy, tools, and talent.

Of all these, your team members' energy level is the one resource that most often gets ignored and yet can have the biggest impact on your success. Don't leave it out of the resource equation.

Instead, check the level of passion or enthusiasm you and your team members have about doing an activity or campaign based on the following five levels of enthusiasm:

- I'm procrastinating—putting this one off as long as possible.
- I'm gritting my teeth—determined to get it done but probably won't enjoy it.
- I'll be happy when it's finished.
- I'm enjoying the journey/process and looking forward to the destination.
- I'm completely engaged and passionate about this activity from start to finish.

For the tools and talent needed:

- Note the total amount of time you and your team will need to spend on this activity.
- Note the budget you and your team will need to spend on this activity.
- Note the tools and equipment you will need to accomplish the activity. This could be computer time, new software, new equipment, etc.
- Note the number of people needed to complete the activity. Be sure to include outside contractors and vendors as well as employees.

ACTION: Complete the resources checklist in chart 18 and summarize your work on the Marketing Accelerator Canvas in the appendix.

Chart 18: Marketing Resources Checklist

MEDIA/ ACTIVITY	ACTION	PRIORITY	TIME	MONEY	TOOLS	TALENT
Website						
Search Engine Marketing; Keyword Optimization						
Internet Marketing; Web Banner Ads						
Workshops/ Webinars						
Social Media Postings; LinkedIn						
Phone Calls						
Email, Drip or Direct						
Conferences						
Event Sponsorship						
Guest Speaking						
Books/ebooks						
Direct Mail; Post Cards						
Referral Program						

Once completed, your Marketing Accelerator Canvas will look something like this.

Figure 25: Example Marketing Accelerator Canvas

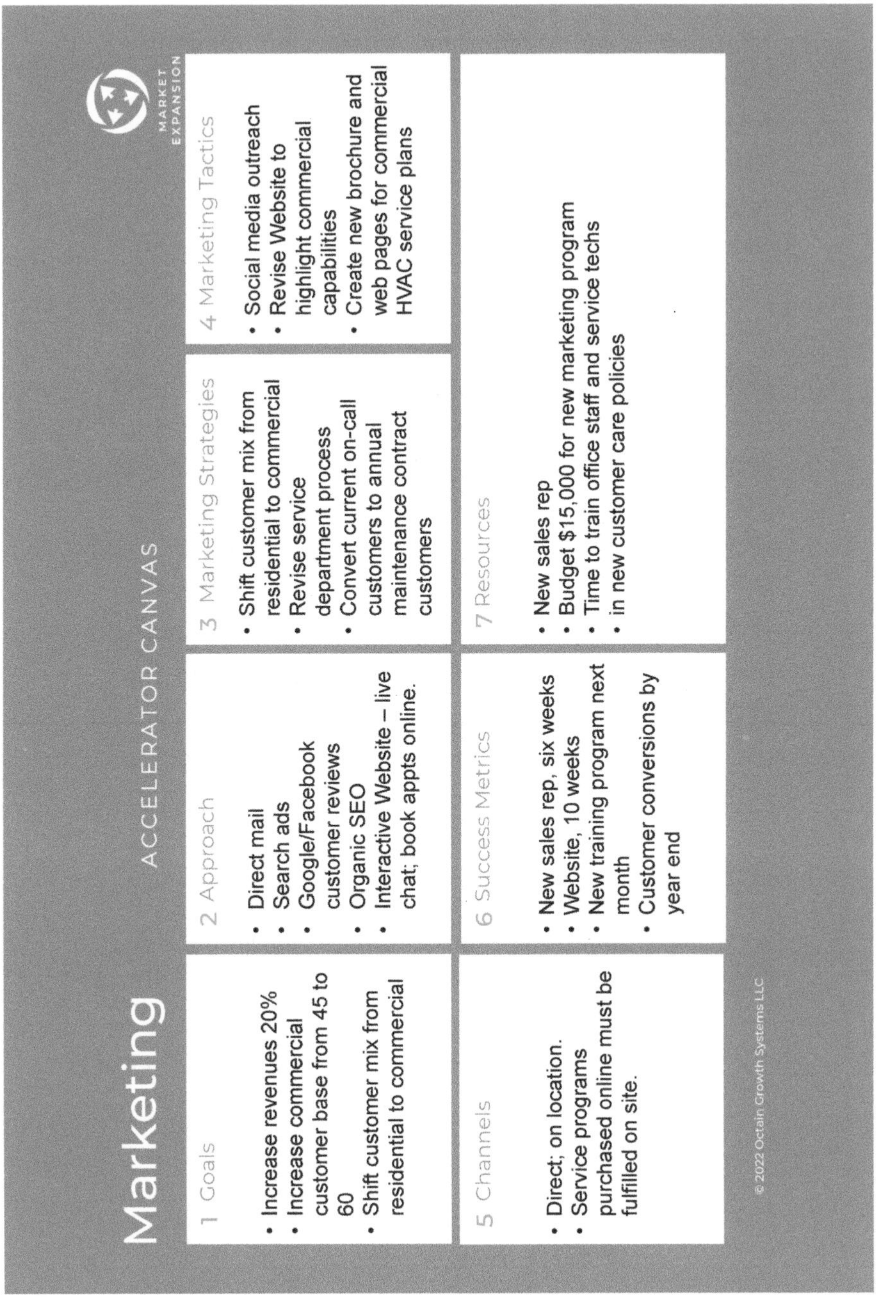
Marketing
ACCELERATOR CANVAS
MARKET EXPANSION
1 Goals
• Increase revenues 20%
• Increase commercial customer base from 45 to 60
• Shift customer mix from residential to commercial
2 Approach
• Direct mail
• Search ads
• Google/Facebook customer reviews
• Organic SEO
• Interactive Website – live chat; book appts online.
3 Marketing Strategies
• Shift customer mix from residential to commercial
• Revise service department process
• Convert current on-call customers to annual maintenance contract customers
4 Marketing Tactics
• Social media outreach
• Revise Website to highlight commercial capabilities
• Create new brochure and web pages for commercial HVAC service plans
5 Channels
• Direct; on location.
• Service programs purchased online must be fulfilled on site.
6 Success Metrics
• New sales rep, six weeks
• Website, 10 weeks
• New training program next month
• Customer conversions by year end
7 Resources
• New sales rep
• Budget $15,000 for new marketing program
• Time to train office staff and service techs
• in new customer care policies
© 2022 Octain Growth Systems LLC

Keys To Market Acceleration

- Determine your business goals for the planning year. Go beyond revenue and profit goals and include specific marketing, customer acquisition, brand, employee, and partner/vendor goals.
- Determine the best market approach for your business goals. For most business builders, a focus on inbound marketing for lead generation will provide the best ROI.
- Develop your marketing strategies by reviewing your strategic marketing options, evaluating your current marketing strengths, and determining the optimum marketing mix.
- Develop your marketing tactics by reviewing the top performing tactics outlined in the chapter, matching your tactics to marketing objectives and the customer response cycle to ensure you have fully addressed the customer journey.
- Choose your best distribution channels and eliminate those you might currently be trying that do not fit your newly developed strategy.
- Allocate resources based on the resource checklist by goal and marketing priority.

ACTION: **Use the example Marketing Accelerator Canvas in the appendix as a guide to summarize all your ideas, insights, and decisions on the Marketing Accelerator Canvas.**

You can find more tools and resources in our OGS Marketing Accelerator Toolbox on our website at www.octaingrowth.com

Chapter 7
SALES ENABLEMENT

Stop selling. Start helping.—Zig Ziglar

FINGER-POINTING. NASTY EMAILS. Overheated meetings. That was the story of an HVAC marketing and sales team in total meltdown because they could not get along. CEO Paulo Freire was ready to fire them all and start over with a new team. However, Freire was just as much a part of the problem, pitting the teams against each other in the erroneous belief that creating "competition" was a successful path to growth.

He was proven wrong. Working through the sales accelerator canvas showed Freire and his sales and marketing executives the importance of cooperation and support. They learned that aligning marketing and sales as an integrated unit was the way to smart marketing execution.

The sales accelerator canvas gives marketing teams the strategies, tactics, process, and tools for effective sales enablement through the alignment of the sales and marketing teams.

Sales Enablement Requires Alignment

It's all about sales. The overarching goal of the OGS is to accelerate sales, revenues, and profits for your business.

That happens when sales is supported so the team can perform more effectively. Sales enablement happens through marketing and sales alignment. These two terms are often used interchangeably because they have a similar purpose and utility with regard to their effect on the bottom line.

Yet they are different. Understanding the difference is important to developing the best structure for your organization.

Sales enablement refers to the systems, processes, tools, and talent that help salespeople do their jobs more effectively to achieve their goals and peak performance. Marketing's role in sales enablement is to support sales.

By contrast, *sales and marketing alignment* is based around a shared system of communication, strategy, and goals that enable marketing and sales to operate as a unified organization. By working together, aligned marketing and sales teams can deliver higher profits, revenues, and performance with a higher impact across the organization.

In short, sales enablement is about higher performing sales teams. Sales and marketing alignment is about organizational success through sales and marketing collaboration and cooperation.

Sales acceleration occurs because of a depth of sales and marketing alignment at the highest levels.

"It's critically important that sales and marketing are aligned because they're both communicating to prospects, and you can't have inconsistency. So when marketing is creating awareness, there needs to be consistency with how sales is communicating during the sales cycle," said Dino Skerlos, president, outsourced VP of sales, Sustainable Sales Solutions.

The bottom line is this: a group within your organization must be dedicated to sales and marketing alignment.

Sales Acceleration Through Effective Alignment

The sales accelerator canvas was created to help you develop and manage an effective sales and marketing alignment team. It offers seven steps that focus on building a sales enablement team and strategies that foster an understanding of players, team dynamics, resourcing, and measuring success.

This is not going to be easy. In most organizations, deep and historic mistrust exists between marketing and sales. And for good reasons: management, goals and compensation, culture, and even personalities are different between the two groups.

People attracted to marketing tend to be creative communicators, great talkers, and team players who see the forest (full of prospects) instead of the trees.

People attracted to sales tend to be self-motivated, deal-focused, great listeners, and individualists who see the tree (with the best fruit) instead of the forest.

Can opposites attract and learn to work together in peace and harmony for mutual success? They can. Accelerated growth depends on it. It starts at the top with the CEO and marketing and sales leadership determined to make it happen.

"Sales and marketing need to be joined at the hip. The sales VP and CMO or the VP of marketing, respecting each other and being connected on what the mission is," said Tim Armstrong, founder and principal, Riptide Sales Advisory, LLC.

Want to kill any chance of sales and marketing alignment? Use the team-of-rivals style of leadership that pits executives and department heads against each other, all vying for prizes like more budget dollars, recognition, and career opportunities.

Success means replacing rivalry with rewarding cooperation and teamwork. Not just with words, which we hear all the time. But in real action within your company management team, compensation plans, operational structure, and most importantly, your leadership and culture.

The sales accelerator canvas was designed to do exactly that.

Figure 26: Octain Sales Accelerator Canvas

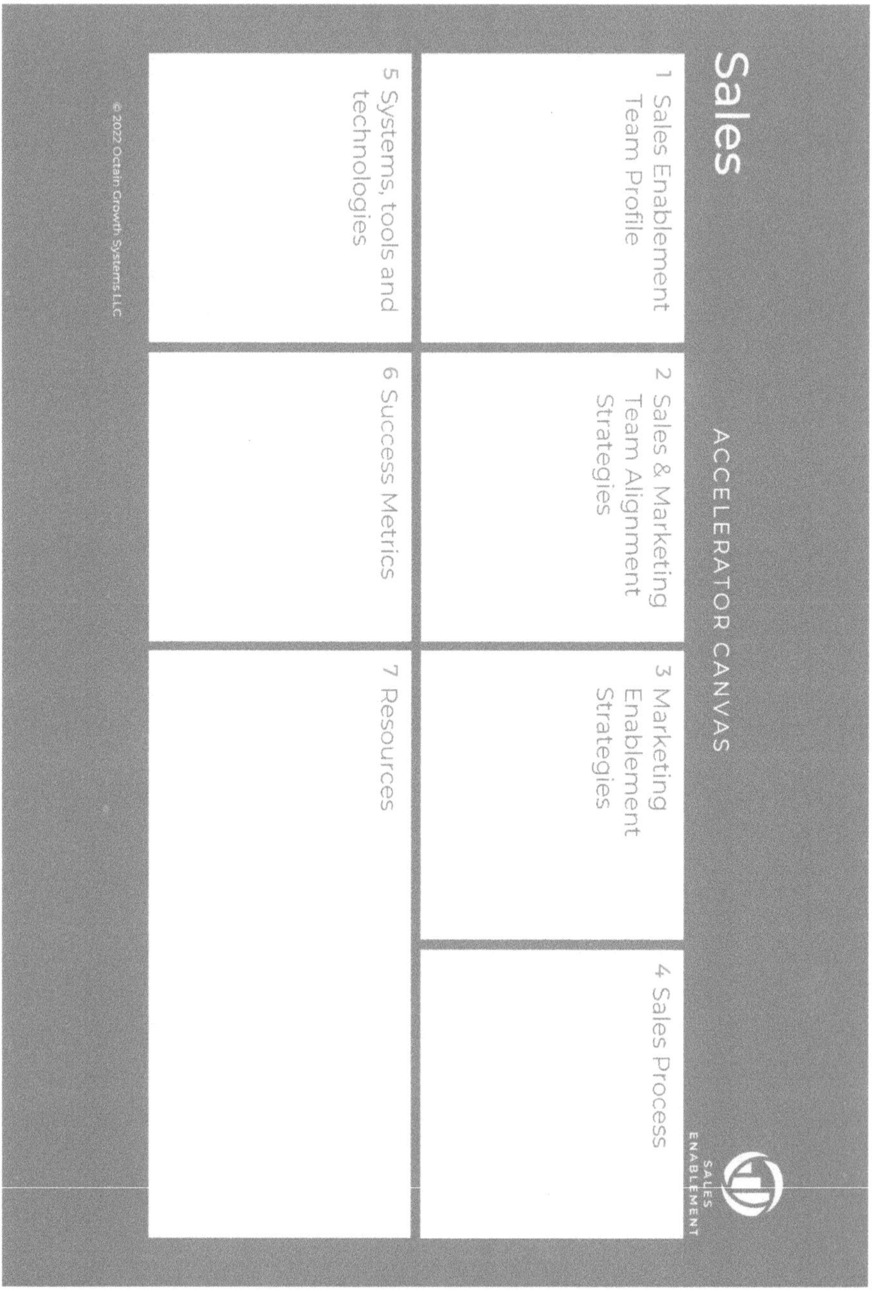
Sales
ACCELERATOR CANVAS
1 Sales Enablement Team Profile
2 Sales & Marketing Team Alignment Strategies
3 Marketing Enablement Strategies
4 Sales Process
5 Systems, tools and technologies
6 Success Metrics
7 Resources
SALES ENABLEMENT
© 2022 Octain Growth Systems LLC

Within OGS, the seven steps to sales and marketing alignment success are:

1. *Sales Enablement Team Profile*—Developing a sales enablement team
2. *Sales and Marketing Team Alignment Strategies*—Creating best practices for team alignment
3. *Marketing Enablement Strategies*—Helping marketing enhance sales success
4. *Sales Process*—Supporting alignment through understanding
5. *Systems, Tools, and Technologies*—Supporting marketing and sales alignment
6. *Success Metrics*—Determining how to measure ROI
7. *Resources*—Identifying the time, money, energy, talent, and tools to be provided by marketing for sales success

Step 1: Develop Sales Enablement Team Profile

Dedication to sales enablement needs to be the core focus of your team of marketing and sales professionals.

Team members recruited to this new business function within the organization should recognize this as an honor and a stepping-stone to higher visibility and career opportunities rather than something that might sideline their organizational progress.

At the same time, as noted below, there are some top performers who will typically not be a fit for your alignment team.

Here are the leadership, culture, and personality traits that work well:

- *Mindset*—Possessing a consultancy mindset that serves an internal audience. Look for people who are dedicated to the strategic elevation of the sales team and are eager to work cooperatively.

- *Personality*—Curious, creative, empathic. Look for empathetic people who clearly understand the audiences they serve. Choose people who are collaborative and willing to embrace the group effort.
- *Expertise*—Select subject matter experts who have a deep understanding of the market, buyers, and technical audiences from a marketing and sales perspective.
- *Education and Experience*—All team members should have a minimum of seven years of professional experience in a similar industry and role to what they will have on your team. A bonus is education and/or credentials in a specific discipline such as B2B or digital marketing.
- *Function Heads*—Choose mature marketing and sales leaders/contributors, ideally those who have worked in both areas and specialized in one.

The alignment team should be composed of equal numbers of sales and marketing professionals—at minimum, two of each, with a maximum of four of each. Other contributors to include on the alignment team are a content/social marketing manager, customer service manager, and IT/operations manager.

It is best to avoid high-performing lone rangers like rainmakers, who meet goals and sales targets and typically have little patience for negotiation, compromise, and conciliatory thinking.

"I want someone who understands the customer and who has enough of an open mind to be able to hear customer feedback and work it backwards into marketing messages," said Deb Brown Maher, sales coach and author of *Sell Like Jesus*.

ACTION: Complete the sales enablement team profile section of the Sales Accelerator Canvas in the appendix.

Step 2: Use Best Practices For Marketing And Sales Team Alignment Strategies

Once the team has been chosen, the next step is to ensure its members have a clear process using best practices.

After working with hundreds of sales and marketing professionals, the following best practices have risen to the top:

Have shared goals and shared responsibility for meeting them. Team alignment starts with that very first meeting to decide mission, goals, and responsibilities. Be prepared to work through differences and disconnects. Don't move forward with the development of the function and business unit until these are satisfactorily resolved.

Have a clear understanding of roles and responsibilities. This goes for each member of the team. It can be helpful to develop written descriptions for everyone that the entire team can review and accept.

Develop specific communication and meeting guidelines. Things to consider here are when and how often the team should meet, how information should be shared, and how to address and resolve differences. The omission of these seemingly small practices can derail a team quickly, so the best time to consider them is before the team gets into day-to-day operations.

These two practices can help with developing guidelines:

- *Institute Service Level Agreements (SLAs)* around the metrics the team will be responsible for. The benefits of an alignment SLA include agreement on quantitative goals and clear expectations on performance and accountability.
- *Formalize your feedback loop.* One of the biggest communication challenges for marketing and sales is how to provide effective feedback in areas like content, lead generation, customer experience, and product/service requirements. Marketing tends to think globally, while sales tends to think specifically. Hashing out how feedback will be shared and the expectation of how it will be used makes communication easier for everyone.

> "Make it a habit to always clarify your understanding of what the other person has said. Questions like, 'Let me make sure I understand you. You said this, you're asking for that, is that right? What did I miss? What else do I need to know?' Taking ownership for digging deeper and making sure you understand, not taking things at face value is important, because marketing has a language they use and sales has a language they use and the two need to come together," said Maher.

Your team should accept these, codify them, and agree to follow them. They also need to be measured and compensated on them. They need to know that leadership expects and rewards this behavior.

ACTION: **Develop a marketing-sales SLA like the one below and add it to the Sales and Marketing Team Alignment Strategies section of the Sales Accelerator Canvas.**

Chart 19: Example Service Level Agreement

Marketing Lead(Name/Email/Phone)	Sales Lead (Name/Email/Phone)
Marketing Goals: MQLs Campaign Metrics Conversion Metrics Revenue growth	Sales Goals: SQLs Lead-to-opportunity conversion rate Win rate – increase Revenue growth
Marketing Initiatives	Sales Initiatives
Accountability Budget and Timeframe	Accountability Budget and Timeframe
Accountability Success Metrics	Accountability Success Metrics
Communication/Reporting Process	Communication/Reporting Process
Marketing Lead Signed	Sales Lead Signed

Step 3: Develop Marketing Enablement Strategies

Did you know? On average, 80 percent of content created by marketers goes unused by B2B salespeople.[19]

Marketing enablement, the Gemini twin of sales enablement, is a critical component of sales and marketing alignment, yet it is often overlooked or ignored. That's a mistake that creates a gaping hole in many sales and marketing alignment departments.

Before marketing can be aligned with sales and foster enablement, the marketing team must have the education, training, experience, and tools to do the job.

Within OGS, marketing enablement is defined as *the process through which marketing-driven functions such as competitive analysis, messaging, content creation and distribution, buyer's journey mapping, and demand generation are used to enhance sales and marketing alignment.*

Effectiveness requires team members with the appropriate education, training, and experience. As noted in the first step on team profiles, the marketing team members should have a minimum of seven years of professional experience in a similar industry and role to what they will have on your team. A bonus is education and/or credentials in a specific discipline such as B2B or digital marketing.

Steps For Developing A Marketing Enablement Strategy

1. Determine the best marketing team members for supporting sales enablement.
2. Complete a content audit with sales alignment partners and review, rank, and score content as to value to the sales cycle.
3. Complete a competitive analysis of the top competitors to arm sales with resources when in competitive bids.
4. Set up competitive company/product alerts to stay on top of breaking news and information that can be quickly pushed out to sales.

5. Develop a sales playbook with sales alignment partners that covers sales stages and definitions, product/service benefits and features, customer personas, and competitor profiles.
6. Develop a lead scoring system that identifies and tracks leads from marketing origin through nurturing to hand off to sales.
7. Map all marketing content to the sales cycle to make sure marketing is providing the appropriate assets at each point in the cycle.

Chart 20: Marketing Enablement Strategy Checklist

Component	Development Timeline (average)	Team Lead	Resources Required For Completion (worksheets in Sales Accelerator Toolbox on our website.)
Choose your marketing enablement team	Three to five days		Marketing team member profiles
Complete an audit of your current content resources	One to four weeks		Content audit worksheet
Complete competitive analysis of top three to five competitors (minimum)	One week per competitor		Competitive analysis spreadsheet
Set up news alerts for companies, products, and top keywords	Two to three hours		Google Alerts or similar alerting program
Develop a sales playbook	Thirty to sixty days		Playbook worksheet
Develop a lead scoring system	One week		Lead scoring worksheet
Map all marketing content to your sales cycle	One week		Content/sales cycle mapping worksheet

Sales and marketing alignment teams really have the chance to shine in the final step: content/sales cycle mapping. The mapping strategy brings together the best capabilities of marketing—content development and sales—to understand prospects and their buying patterns. Figure 27 shows a completed content/sales cycle map.

Figure 27: Content/Sales Cycle Map

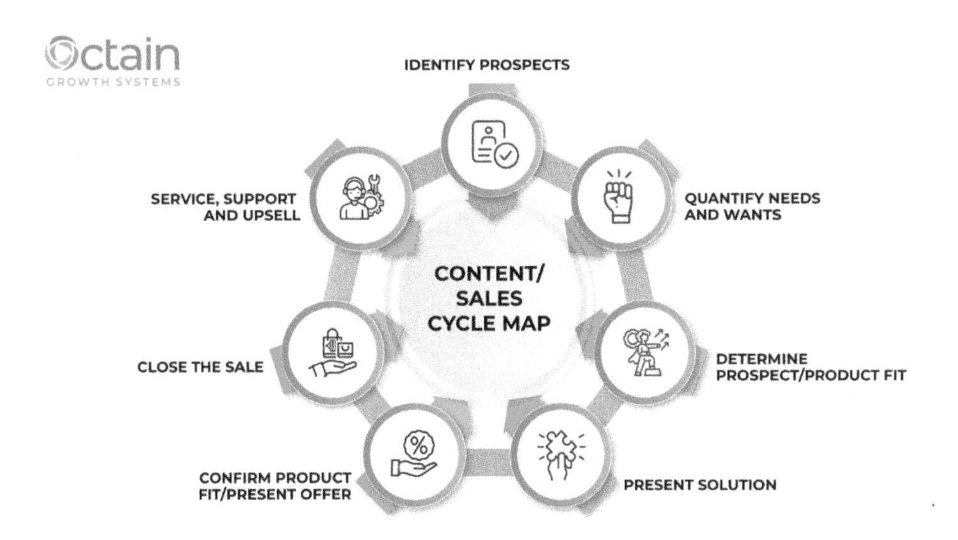

ACTION: Complete the marketing enablement strategy checklist above and the Marketing Enablement Strategies section of the Sales Accelerator Canvas in the appendix.

Step 4: Sales Process: Alignment Through Understanding

To many marketers, the sales process is a mystery. Even if they have had a joint marketing/sales role at some point, their take on the experience is likely to be different. One of the biggest areas of miscommunication, frustration, and finger-pointing between marketing and sales is exactly what is a qualified lead.

"We get very casual when we work together in a company. We think we know what each other means. That's a dangerous position to take," said Deb Brown Maher, author of *Sell Like Jesus*.

"It's always critical to seek clarification and make sure you truly understand each other. Make sure there's agreement, buy-in, and sign-off. This helps avoid the misunderstandings where everybody goes to their corner and does their own thing, only to find out later that they'd missed the mark," Maher added.

The Difference between Marketing and Sales Qualified Leads

Mansur-Nelson Automotive was looking to expand from Northern to Southern California and into Arizona. The marketing team was using a traditional direct mail marketing approach and leads were coming in, but the sales team wasn't closing them.

"Give us more leads," the salespeople demanded.

"Close the leads we are giving you," the marketing people snapped back.

The problem between the two teams was a misunderstanding of what was a qualified lead. It's a common problem, one that can easily be avoided by ensuring the sales and marketing alignment team understands and communicates the difference.

According to the research firm Gartner:

A marketing-qualified lead (MQL) is a potential customer who has been reviewed by the marketing team and satisfies the criteria necessary to be passed along to the sales team.[20]

A sales-qualified lead (SQL) is a prospective customer who has moved through the sales pipeline—from marketing-qualified lead through sales-accepted lead—to a position where the sales team can now work on converting them into an active customer.[21]

The problem starts when marketing passes along unqualified leads such as when someone requests a download. That is usually the very beginning of the buyer's journey, way before that prospect is ready to talk to sales.

Instead of passing that lead to sales, the prospect should be nurtured with additional content and offers designed to move them along the buyer's journey from awareness to consideration as shown in figure 28.

Figure 28: Buyers' Journey With Nurture Content

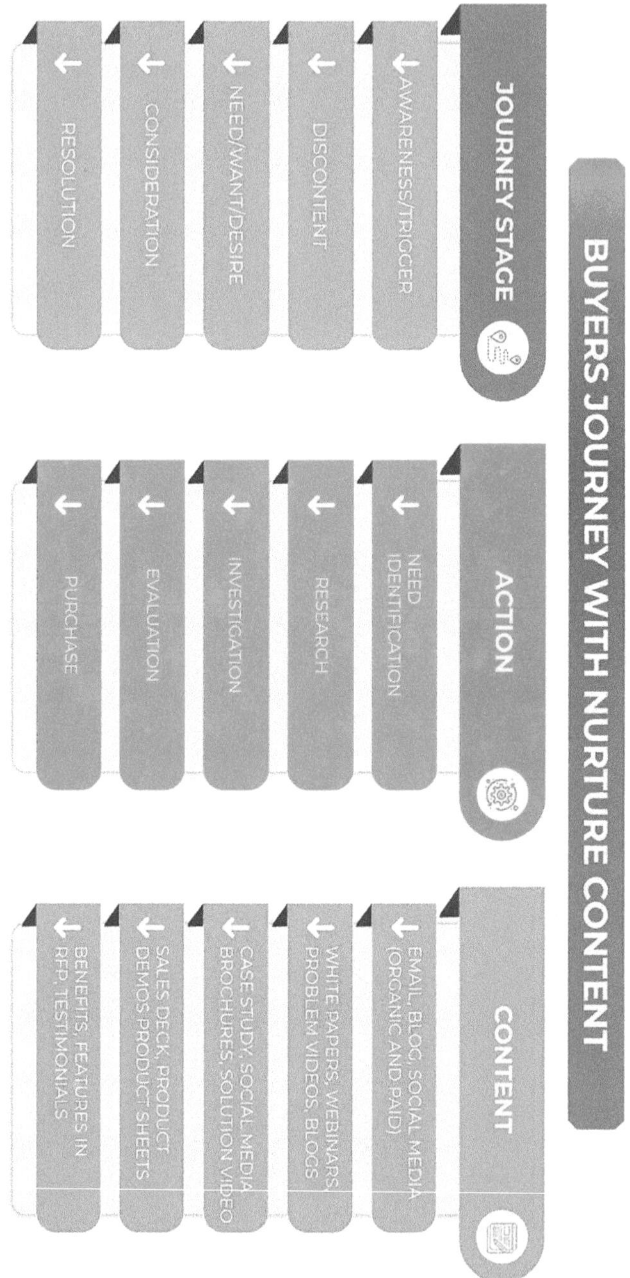

Experience A Day In The Life

What opens marketing people's eyes to the sales life is to experience a day in the life of a sales rep. Tim Armstrong of Riptide suggests ride-alongs.

"The number one thing you need here is for each side to walk a mile in the other's shoes. I like to bring marketing people out into the field on a sales call. And they've had us into their sessions on messaging creation and competitive analysis. You have to walk in each other's shoes so that it's not an adversarial relationship," said Armstrong.

When marketing sits across the table from a prospect and hears the objections and direct questions salespeople are facing, it not only brings new appreciation for the life of the salesperson, it gives the marketer new ideas for content and messaging.

"When really good professionals get together, they learn to think like each other. Marketing will say I am empathetic with your lead gen situation. I can see there's macro changes in the market right now that are going to affect your ability to sell so let's pivot on this right now. When that happens and those leaders that stay connected in that way, that's unstoppable," said Armstrong.

ACTION: Set up sales and marketing ride-alongs so marketing can experience the sales process in real time. Also invite salespeople who are on the alignment team to join the content development process.

Step 5: Systems, Tools, And Technologies

Talent, time, and tools are the pillars of sales and marketing alignment. We covered talent in the first step and time in the fourth by developing an effective alignment process through understanding. Neither of these can succeed without the right tools.

Gartner defines sales enablement platforms (SEPs) as tools that unite sales enablement functions and customer-facing sales execution. They predominantly feature native capabilities for sales content, sales training, and coaching.[22]

Choosing the best tools for your team can be complex and confusing because the sales enablement arena is flooded with them. A look at the basic categories of sales enablement tools will give you an overview of what is available.

Sales enablement tools are based on a system or platform that provides automated support for the entire sales cycle. They include the key components noted in figure 29.

Figure 29: Sales Engagement Platform

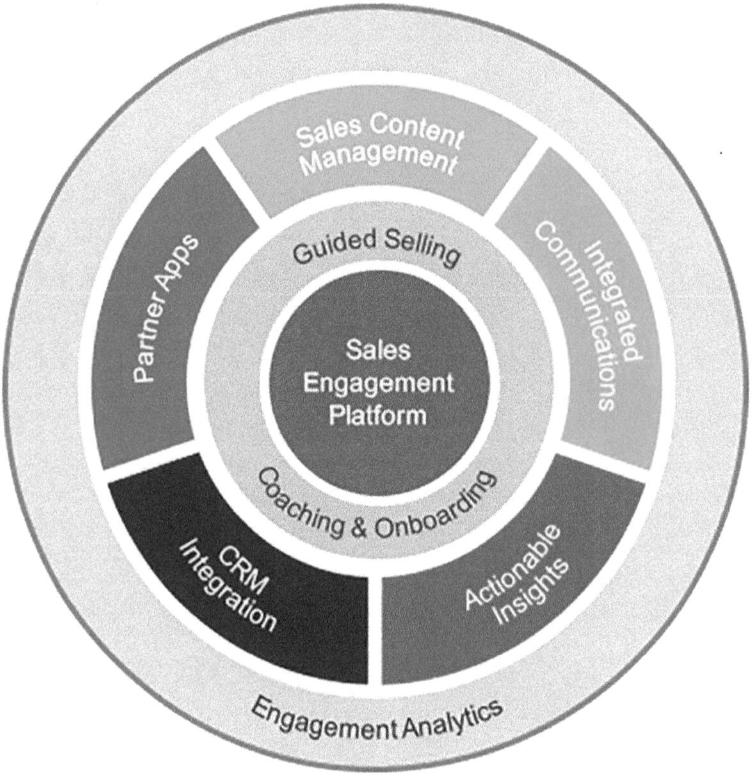

Source: Clearslide, http://www.clearslide.com

To choose the most effective sales enablement system for your company's needs, determine system requirements after the alignment team has been chosen. Their location, working styles, roles, and responsibilities will have a big impact on the system requirements.

Six leading-edge, innovative sales enablement vendors worth a look are listed in Chart 21.

Chart 21: Innovative Sales Enablement Vendors

Company	Key Functionality	Website
Seismic	Seismic's Storytelling Platform™ enables marketers to deliver relevant content across all channels to engage with prospective buyers at every step of the buyer journey.	https://seismic.com/
Showpad	Revenue enablement software that provides every customer-facing team with the required skills, knowledge, content, and tools to have differentiating, impactful conversations with buyers and customers.	https://www.showpad.com/
Highspot	Enablement platform that empowers companies to elevate customer conversations for strategic growth. Platform combines intelligent content management, contextual guidance, training, rep coaching, and customer engagement with end-to-end analytics and AI.	https://www.highspot.com/
ClearSlide	Sales enablement platform that provides sales content, communications, and insights for sales teams. By mapping high-value ClearSlide engagement interaction between sellers and buyers, leaders can instantly see which deals are on track or may be at risk.	https://www.clearslide.com/
Mediafly	Platform offers sales enablement, content and digital asset management, sales training and coaching, analytics, and revenue intelligence for sales teams.	https://www.mediafly.com/
Gong	To provide revenue intelligence, Gong captures and analyzes customer interactions and alerts you to risks and opportunities across your business by capturing communications, analyzing the data, and delivering insights.	https://www.gong.io/

ACTION: Evaluate your current systems and tools for usability, performance, and capability. Consider contacting an automation partner to help perform an audit of your current systems and tools and provide recommendations for improvements.

Step 6: Success Metrics

Too often, business owners and marketers use one metric to measure the success of all their programs: did we make or lose money?

While that top-line number is critical, it is not enough, because it often hides missteps in other areas that left unchecked will eventually hit your top- and bottom-line revenues and profits. It can also cover up problems team members are having that, if quickly identified and addressed, can dramatically improve program success.

You can avoid those issues with this simple performance scorecard that tracks the key metrics that highlight performance successes and challenges.

A monthly rolling scorecard may provide the best results.

Chart 22: Sales Enablement Scorecard

Team Metrics	Target Goal	Monthly Target	Last Month Actual	Next Month Projected
Lead-to-opportunity conversion rate				
Win rate—increase				
Competitive win rate				
Average selling price				

Sales cycle length — decrease				
Quota attainment— speed increase				
Content adoption				
KPIs to Track				
Sales call metrics/KPIs				
Number of calls made				
Average time between calls				
Number of leads generated				
Average time to 50, 80, and 100 percent quota				
Number of price quotes generated				

ACTION: Complete the sales enablement scorecard in chart 22 and summarize your answers in the sales metrics section of the Sales Accelerator Canvas.

Step 7: Resources

Look beyond the typical resource requirements of time, talent, and money. In the sales accelerator canvas, resources are what marketing needs to provide to sales to create alignment that leads to sales enablement.

Here's what the top sales leaders we interviewed told us.

"Competitive analysis. Marketing is more focused on what competitors are doing in the news and in tracking their features and functions. It might be a little thing, a small feature and if marketing puts it in a database where sales can get it that is just in time information for sales," said sales consultant Mitch Armstrong.

"Content creation is critical for sales because sales need stories to paint a picture, both in getting the prospect to resonate more with the pain they currently have and to see the benefit of solving those problems. Marketing is in a better position to create those stories," said Dino Skerlos of Sustainable Sales Solutions.

"The number one thing we need is messaging. Everybody has to be wrapped around the same value proposition. What marketing is good at is crystallizing that and making messaging that matters," said Riptide's Tim Armstrong. "From a sales leader perspective, the ones that get right to the buyer journey level and own lead generation. That's the best connective tissue right there."

"Marketing people can't expect salespeople to come to them with messaging messages. Salespeople are going to come with a problem: this customer had this situation and this problem. The marketing person has to be able to ask the salesperson questions, to get the data needed, to reverse engineer those comments into messaging," said sales coach Deb Brown Maher.

In short, marketing should focus on resources in these areas to best align their activities with sales needs in these areas:

- *Competitive analysis.* The importance of competitive analysis cannot be overstated, and it is too often underrated by marketing teams focused on customer analysis. Detailed competitive analysis can help marketing shape messaging and customer offers and position the company in the market space.

Sales sees the competitors when the prospect mentions who else they are evaluating or may be using. They see competitors when they displace them—a major win. Marketing can support sales with a detailed review of the pros and cons of each competitor in relation to their products/services as well their approach/message to the target customer.

- *Messaging.* Sales looks to marketing to provide the overall message and content direction, to use messaging to position the company and offer competitive differentiation.
- *Buyers' journeys.* Here is where marketing can align with sales to have a real impact on sales enablement. Marketing is the primary resource for deciding at what point in the buyer's journey leads should be handed to sales. When it is too early in the buyer's journey, the prospect shuts the door because they are not ready. If the lead is handed off too late, the prospect may have already chosen a competitor.
- *Content.* Content is the vehicle for delivering the message. Marketing should develop the content assets. True alignment comes in when insights from the field are integrated into marketing insights to deliver more relevant sales conversations. The sales enablement platforms reviewed above can be a great asset here and also provide analytics.
- *Analytics.* Today more than ever, data enables effective sales performance. For marketing and sales alignment, usage and engagement analytics are just the beginning. Other key metrics are content usage, buyer interest, sales conversations mapped against conversion, and sales call/cart abandonment.

Chart 23: Sales Enablement Resource Checklist

Sales/ Marketing Enablement Resources	Current Activities	Resources Expended	Success Factors	Experience	Desired Not Done
	Check all you have used in the last twelve to eighteen months.	Note time, people, and budget resources used.	How successful was this activity in reaching your goals? Can rank from 1 (low) to 10 (high).	Please note your positive and negative responses to this activity.	Please check activities you wanted to do but did not do. Note reason this was not done.
Content					
Competitive analysis profiles					
Messaging					
Website					
Email marketing					
Newsletters					
Workshops/ seminars					
Webinars					
Social media					
Blogs/white papers/ ebooks					
Videos					
Mobile marketing					
ADVERTISING					
Coupons					

Sales/ Marketing Enablement Resources	Current Activities	Resources Expended	Success Factors	Experience	Desired Not Done
Pricing specials					
SMS/text ads					
Social media ads					
Search engine marketing (pay per click)					
Internet marketing—web banner ads					
Print Media/ Radio/TV					
Trade shows/ Events					
ANALYTICS					
Google					
Facebook Insights					
Mixpanel					
Google Ads Performance Grader					
Semrush					
CRM/ marketing automation					

ACTION: Complete the sales enablement resource checklist above and be sure to summarize your work on the Sales Accelerator Canvas in the appendix.

Once completed, your sales accelerator canvas will look something like this:

Figure 30: Example Sales Accelerator Canvas

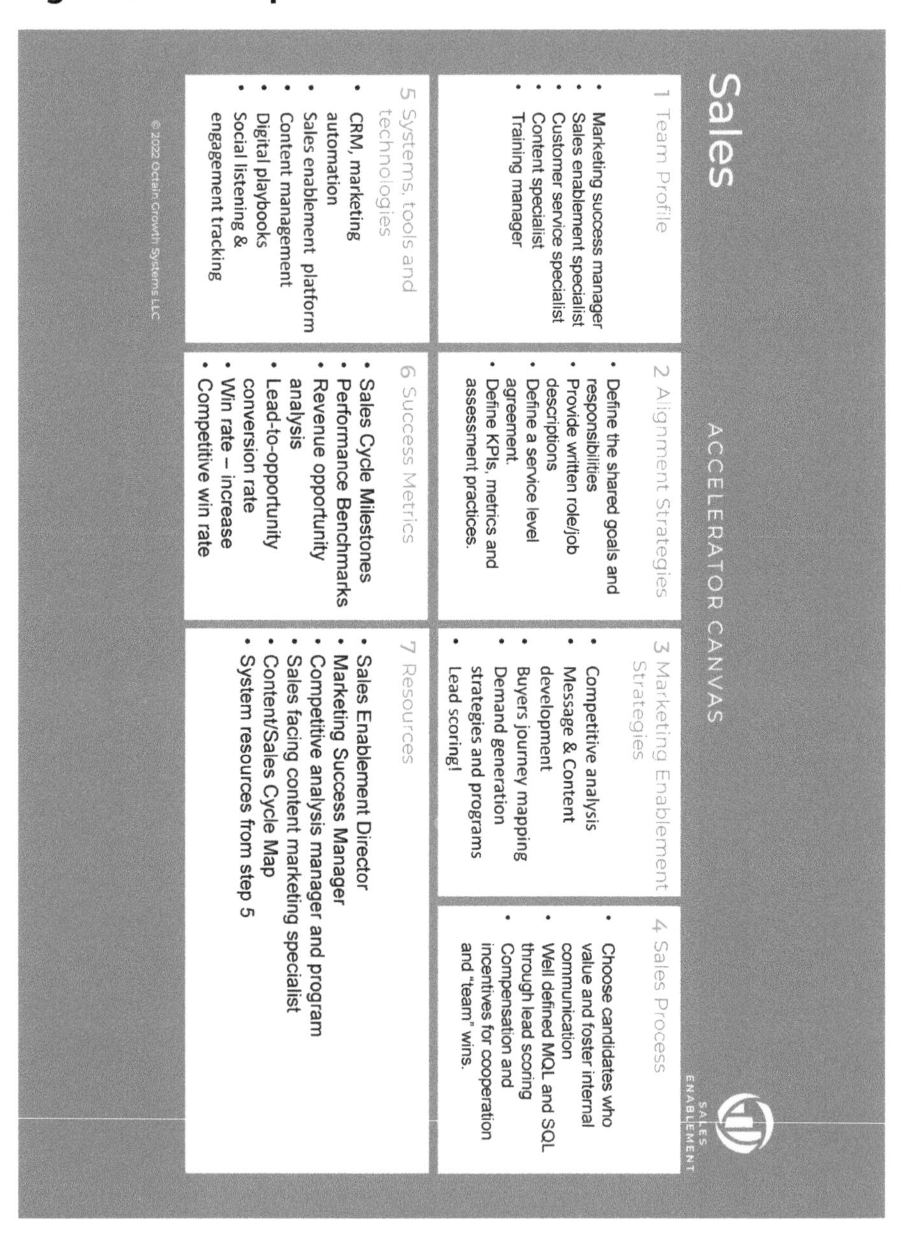

Keys To Sales Acceleration

1. Develop a sales and marketing alignment team/unit within your organization composed of experienced marketing and sales professionals who share the common goal of wanting to collaborate and cooperate to ensure all professionals on both teams succeed.
2. Develop a set of best practices for your organization's alignment team and secure cooperation with an SLA for the team.
3. Develop a market enablement strategy and action plan.
4. Promote understanding between marketing and sales teams by clearly defining the lead qualification and scoring process and creating opportunities for marketing and sales to work more closely together. Encourage marketing and sales ride-alongs.
5. Evaluate your current sales enablement systems and tools. Consider hiring an automation partner to audit your systems, evaluate your needs, and recommend improvements.
6. Develop and institute a set of success metrics. Hold all team members accountable to them on a monthly basis.
7. Use the sales enablement checklist to determine and acquire the resources needed for marketing and sales alignment and sales enablement success.
8. Use the example Sales Accelerator Canvas in the appendix as a guide to summarize all of your ideas, insights, and decisions on the Sales Accelerator Canvas.

You can find more tools and resources for the canvas in the OGS Sales Accelerator Toolbox on our website at www.octaingrowth.com.

Chapter 8
PRODUCT/SERVICE INNOVATION

Marketing's job is never done. It's about perpetual motion. We must continue to innovate every day.— Beth Comstock, Former CMO and Vice Chair, GE

RUBICON BAKERY HAD a transportation problem: vibrations in trucking were causing cupcakes to bounce around and get icing on top of the trays. Revere Packaging solved that problem by designing specialty packaging that "pinned" the cupcake to the bottom of the container, preserving the aesthetics of the cupcake and the container. As a result, they displaced Rubicon's current packaging company and became the bakery's supplier of choice for all plastic packaging.

It's Not Really Product Marketing Unless You Change Things

And for high growth, change them dramatically.

Traditional product marketing is defined as the process of bringing your goods and services to market. No surprise there. Typically, this involves developing the product's positioning and messaging; launching the product; and educating salespeople, the market, and customers about the features and benefits. Too often, it means broadcasting how great the product is for the customer and why they desperately need it.

Within OGS it is done differently. We don't see product marketing as pushing your product out into the market or artificially creating demand that compels customers to buy. We see it as changing the product to first meet, then exceed, and finally—most importantly—anticipate future customer needs so you have what the customer needs available just as they are beginning to look for it.

This is done through the product/service accelerator canvas, which will help your marketing team see your products and services with a new perspective through a different lens.

Figure 31: Product/Service Accelerator Canvas

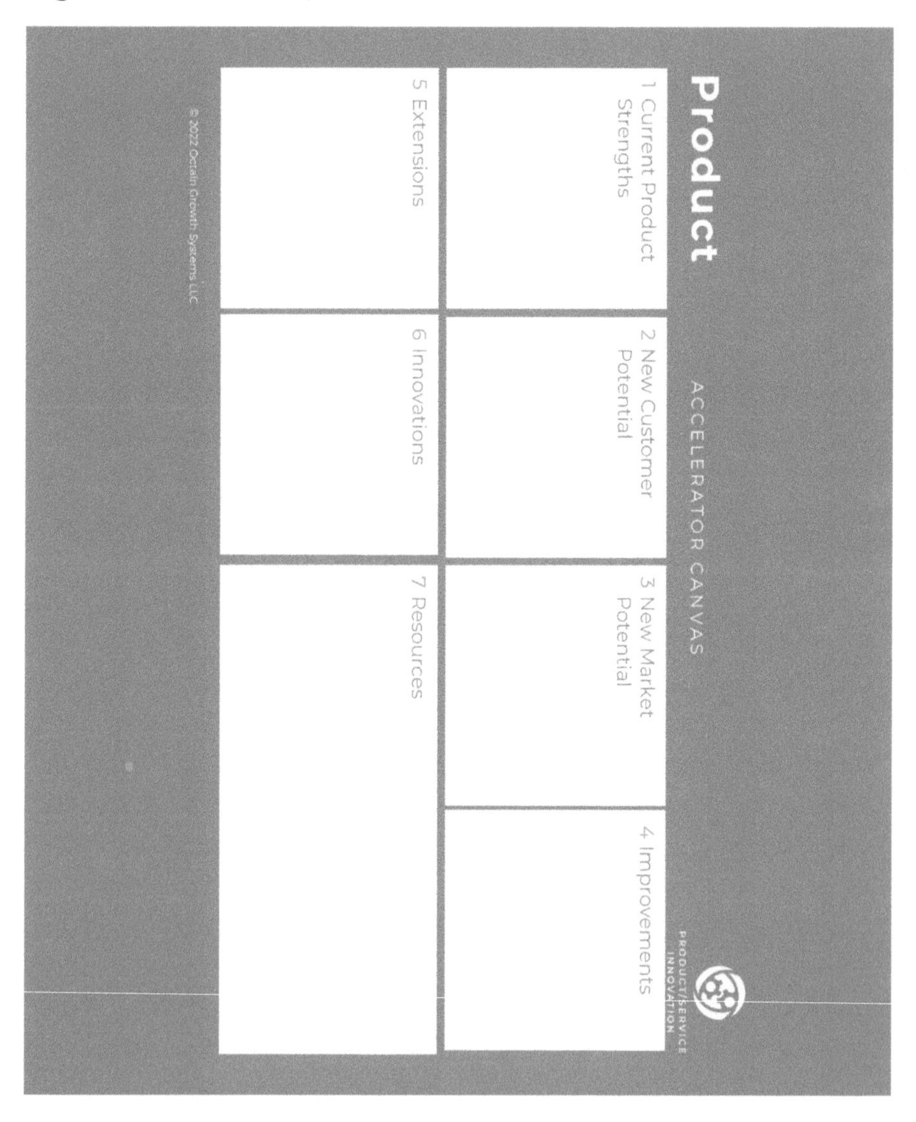

The seven steps of the product/service accelerator canvas are:

1. *Current Product Strengths*—Used to assess your current product strengths to determine the competitive and market strengths of your product or services.
2. *New Customer Potential*—Used to help your team find new customer groups for your products and services.
3. *New Market Potential*—Used to help your team discover how your product/service strengths can be used in a new niche.
4. *Improvements*—Used to determine how you can make your product/service easier to use, more affordable, or faster to get customer results.
5. *Extensions*—Used to determine how you can expand your product/service capabilities or customer reach to attract new customers or industry segments.
6. *Innovations*—Used to discover ways you can push the boundaries of your current product/service focus and overcome limitations to expand your market presence.
7. *Resources*—Used to map out what it will take in time, talent, money, systems, and tools to accomplish your new product/service goals.

Step 1: Evaluate Your Current Strengths

Use the worksheet below to determine the competitive and market strengths of your product or service. Consider how you can use these strengths to compete better in today's digital economy.

Chart 24: Product/Service Strength Finder Matrix

Product/Service Strengths	Market Penetration	Competitive Advantage	Upsell Potential	New Customer Potential	New Market Potential
Why our product/ service is purchased. What it is known for. EXAMPLES: Ease of Use, Customization, Personalized Service	Based on this strength, how many potential customers have we successfully sold it to?	Does this feature help us compete more effectively or less effectively for new sales?	Does this strength enable us to sell more of what we have to existing customers? Volume, related products, etc.	How can this strength be used to appeal to different segments or types of customers?	How can this strength be used to appeal to more of the same kind of customers in other areas?
Ease of Use	Start-up able to achieve 15 percent saleable available market (SAM) due to AI-driven automation built into product design	Start-up has a 60 percent success rate in displacing existing competitors in California EdTech market	Continuing automation enhancements requested by current customers deliver double-digit increase in seats purchased	Start-up able to expand from education market into city, community market segment	Start-up expanded product line from website development to mobile app development

ACTION: Complete the product/service strength finder matrix chart in chart 24, above, and summarize it in the current product strengths section of the Product Accelerator Canvas in the appendix.

Step 2: Determine Your New Customer Potential

Even if you have lots of room to grow your current customer base, it is wise to serve at least three different market segments.

New customer segments can protect you against roller-coaster buying cycles. If more customers buy your product in the summer and winter is a slow season, find a segment that needs your product in your current slow season and smooth out your revenue generation.

New customer segments protect and expand your market penetration. Customer dynamics are always changing. Customer needs and desires change. Markets can blow up, especially in today's volatile times.

The 2020 COVID-19 lockdowns killed indoor restaurant dining. The restaurants that survived and thrived found new customer segments—not only shifting from indoor dining to takeout but by doing innovative things like starting food trucks. Instead of waiting for customers to walk in the door, chefs like Erick Johnson of The Chef's Table in Rocklin, California, served gourmet meals in his parking lot.

In the Great Recession of 2007-2009, the real estate industry collapsed almost overnight. Traditional buyers and sellers disappeared, and many real estate agents got out of the business. One client became a casino marketer at Thunder Valley Casino in Lincoln, California. One became a schoolteacher.

Another of my very successful six-figure agents, who had a four-person team in Roseville, California, refused to give up on the real estate market. He became a foreclosure expert, helping distressed homeowners navigate the new world of selling their homes at a loss, something unheard of in California at that time.

To find potential new customers for your products and services, start with the customer profiles/personas you built using the customer canvas. Let's say your current high value target customer is a manufacturing CEO.

Your persona probably looks something like this:

High Driver and High I on the DiSC profile: extroverted and outgoing and task-oriented. They are influencers who tend to be direct, decisive, driven, and demanding.

- responds well to facts and figures
- big picture thinking
- buying concern—cost of ownership, cost of failure
- buying concern—business disruption
- buying decision—cost-benefit analysis
- buying decision—ROI
- buying decision—team productivity impact

The sales problem-solving opportunity looks like this:

- needs to improve customer service
- competitors expanding into key markets
- needs to reduce cost to serve markets
- needs to support a disparate workforce, processes, and systems

Next, consider what other customer types might have similar characteristics and problems to the one you are profiling in your canvas. For example, CEOs in segments that face similar challenges to manufacturing like logistics, construction, and hardware technology. Make a list of other C-suite executives like the CFO or Chief Information Officer (CIO) in the same or related industries that also might be good candidates for your products/services.

ACTION: Use the Customer Accelerator Canvas in chapter 3 to build out new personas and see how they align with your current customer base.

Step 3: Determine Your New Market Potential

It is nearly impossible to accelerate your growth as a mid-market company without finding new markets. The more successful you are in your current market, the stronger the urge to stay put and heavily work it, especially if your current market penetration is small and there is plenty of room to grow.

However, the more entrenched you are in one or two markets, the more devastating it is when those markets change. And they will. That happened to me in the Great Recession of 2007–2009, with my business that focused on real estate marketing and branding. Boom! Like my clients, my business virtually disappeared overnight. I'll never forget going to see one of my Keller Williams clients and seeing the doors to Financial Title Company, a major force in the Sacramento real estate market, chain locked with a closure notice posted.

Needless to say, I had to find a new market segment to serve, and fast. I used the niche discovery checklist in figure 32, below, approach to find my new niche.

Figure 32: Niche Discovery Checklist

As you can see, a simple way to begin to discover new market potential is to start from your established market and look for other customer types, industries, or segments that share these characteristics. If, for example, your product has a strong presence in manufacturing, could it also serve the construction industry?

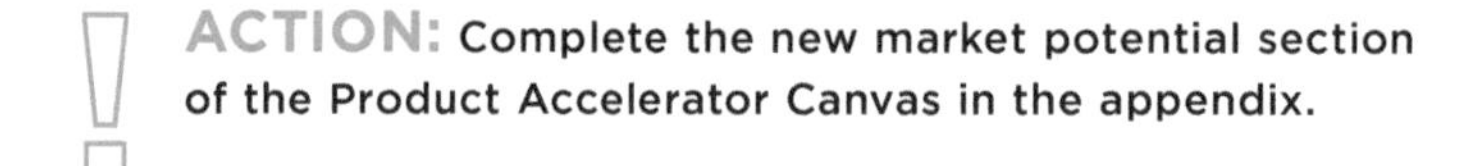

ACTION: Complete the new market potential section of the Product Accelerator Canvas in the appendix.

Map Your Possibilities

Once you have evaluated your current product/service strengths and determined your new market and customer potential, it is time to consider product/service changes that will help you accelerate your growth in these new opportunities.

For that we begin with my favorite tool, the mind map.

It's time to blue-sky how you might rethink, reinvent, and innovate your products and services for today's economy. One of the best ways to do that is with a mind map. To get you started, mine is in figure 33, created in Whimsical.[23]

Another resource you may want to consider is an online collaborative whiteboard platform like Miro.[24]

Figure 33: Mind Map

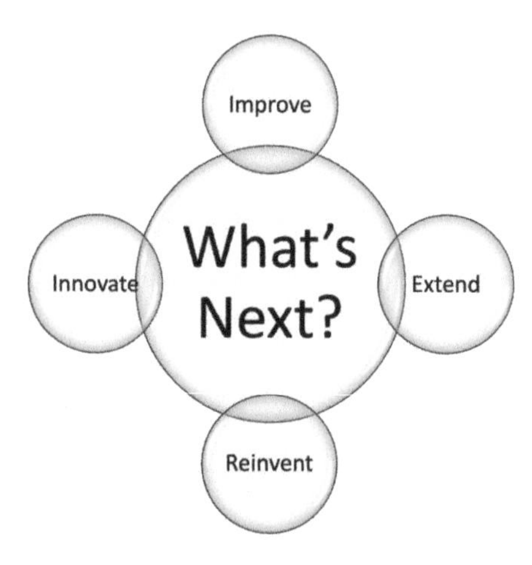

Note the four categories:

1. Improve—How can you make your product/service easier to use, more affordable, or faster to get customer results?
2. Extend—How can you expand your product/service capabilities or customer reach?
3. Reinvent—How can your product/service solve a related problem or serve another customer group?
4. Innovate—What can you do to push the boundaries of your current product/service focus and limitations? What's the one crazy thing you can do (that may seem impossible today) to better serve your market and customers?

Each of these categories requires a new perspective and a willingness to step beyond your current activity. Which one are you willing to step into today? And how do you decide what steps to take first?

We explore that in steps four to seven of the product/service brand accelerator canvas.

Step 4: How to Improve Your Products or Services

This can be a small incremental step that should be fast, easy, and inexpensive to complete.

Chart 25 is a quick worksheet to determine the best ways to improve your products/services for immediate market benefit.

Chart 25: Product/Service Improvement Worksheet

Feature/Function	Customer/Market Benefit (Why?)	Resource Cost	Expected ROI	Priority
Easier to use				
More affordable				
Faster/better results				

One fatal mistake I've seen over and over again is assuming as a product marketing team that you "know" what the market/customers want. Another big one is ignoring sales input. It's easy to avoid those two mistakes.

Start by directly asking your customers what they want next. Get out and talk to them face-to-face or directly in a video conference where you can ask follow-up questions. Do not rely on surveys; instead, use them as a guide to choose the best customers to interview. Of course, everyone wants to talk to happy customers, but you often learn much more from unhappy customers, especially those who have switched from your company to a competitor.

Ask sales. They are on the frontlines and they know. Ask customer service reps, especially those who monitor phones or chats. They know too.

Don't make this exercise a one-time thing. Instead, maintain a feature/function database with everything a customer might be looking for in the future. This is standard in the tech space. But it can apply to just about every product and even services.

If a customer mentions something even in casual conversation they do or do not like/want/need, whether it directly relates to your current product/service or not, capture it and maintain it in a database.

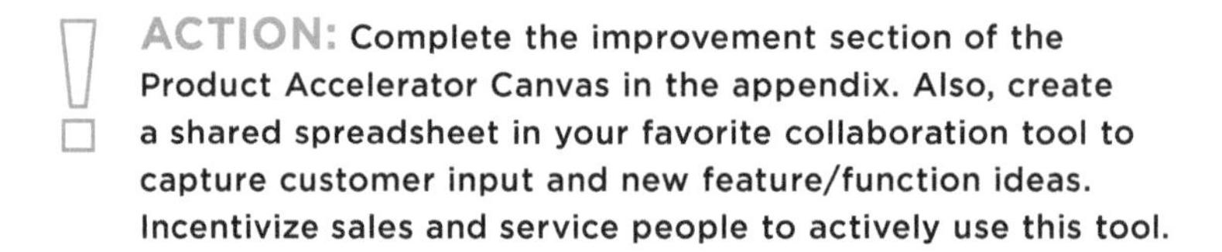

Step 5: How To Extend Your Products and Services

Product line extensions are a time-honored way large consumer brands accelerate their growth. By launching a new version of an existing product with new features, functions, and services you allow current customers to do more with it. You can also find new customers in a related market segment.

Product extensions:

- offer current customers more choices and variety
- encourage replacing and upgrading existing products
- deepen customer loyalty
- introduce your products and services to new customers and markets
- create a new competitive advantage
- create market excitement and buzz

A SaaS client had maxed out its current market niche. It was the recognized leader in the space and the go-to company for process mapping software in the construction space in its local market. The company wasn't going to find the 28 percent revenue growth per quarter it sought with its current offering and market niche.

Using the OGS discovery process, the executive management team decided to extend the product in two successful ways. First, they modified the software mapping process to make the software more useful for architects, the head of their construction customer supply chain. Second, they added a new app to the mapping software to make it more useful on the job. The result was a quarterly jump in sales of 32 percent, beating their revenue goal.

To discover ways your company can extend its product/service line, start with the questions:

- What will let our products/services do more for existing customers?
- Who else could our product serve?
- Where else could people/communities use our product/services?

ACTION: Complete the extension section of the Product Accelerator Canvas in the appendix.

Step 6: How To Innovate Your Products And Services

Innovation, finding that new method, product, or idea that opens up new doors and opportunities in a time of turmoil, is your crisis protection plan. Innovation is not an activity. Innovation is a mindset.

It's a mindset that is willing to look at every component of your business with a new perspective. It's a mindset that questions everything, especially the tried-and-true. When innovation works, it's a little scary on its own—even more so now with all the other upheavals your team is dealing with. At the same time, embracing innovation has gotten easier, because we all know what we are used to doing won't work today as it has in the past.

The OGS approach to the innovation mindset is threefold: identify strengths, develop a mind map, and create a blueprint for implementation.

A mature software company was trapped in an aging market space with little growth potential. Several new products were suggested but none were innovative. They were all safe bets. No one was happy. Using the product/service accelerator canvas and the innovation questions in the mind map, the executive team was able to identify the best ROI-based options for their company.

With stakeholder agreement, the choice was narrowed to one—launch an upgrade in a new market space—something that opened a new geographic market, changed the company's competitive position, and drove new sales growth of 24 percent in the first twelve months following the launch.

To discover ways your company can innovate your products and services, start with the questions:

- How can we push the boundaries of our current technology, approach, or service?
- What market shifts are emerging that we can innovate to meet?
- What's the one crazy thing we can do (that may seem impossible today) to better serve our market and customers?

ACTION: Complete the innovation section of your mind map and be sure to summarize your work on the canvas.

Step 7: Determine Your Resource Requirements

What resources (time, money, tools, and talent) your team has and how well they use them determines what you can accomplish.

Use this product marketing worksheet to help determine what improvements, extensions, and innovations will give your company the best ROI.

Chart 26: Product/Service Resource Requirement Matrix

FEATURE/ FUNCTION	OBJECTIVE	CUSTOMER OPPORTUNITY	MARKET OPPORTUNITY	BUILD REQUIREMNTS
TIME TOTAL				
TIME UNIT				
MONEY TOTAL				
MONEY UNIT				
TOOLS				
TALENT				

Also, take advantage of these community resources for product marketing support:

The Product Marketing Alliance[25] is an aggregated site of product marketing education, community support, and resources for continued professional product marketing development.

Product Marketing World[26] is an ongoing series of physical and digital summits created by product marketers for product marketers. Summits take place throughout the year in many global locations.

Sharebird[27] describes itself as a "Q&A site for product marketers." This online forum focused on product marketing topics offers product marketing advice from product marketers at Adobe, Salesforce, Airbnb, and many other corporate leaders.

ACTION: Complete the product/service resource checklist and be sure to summarize your work on the Product Acceleration Canvas in the appendix.

Figure 34: Completed Product/Service Accelerator Canvas

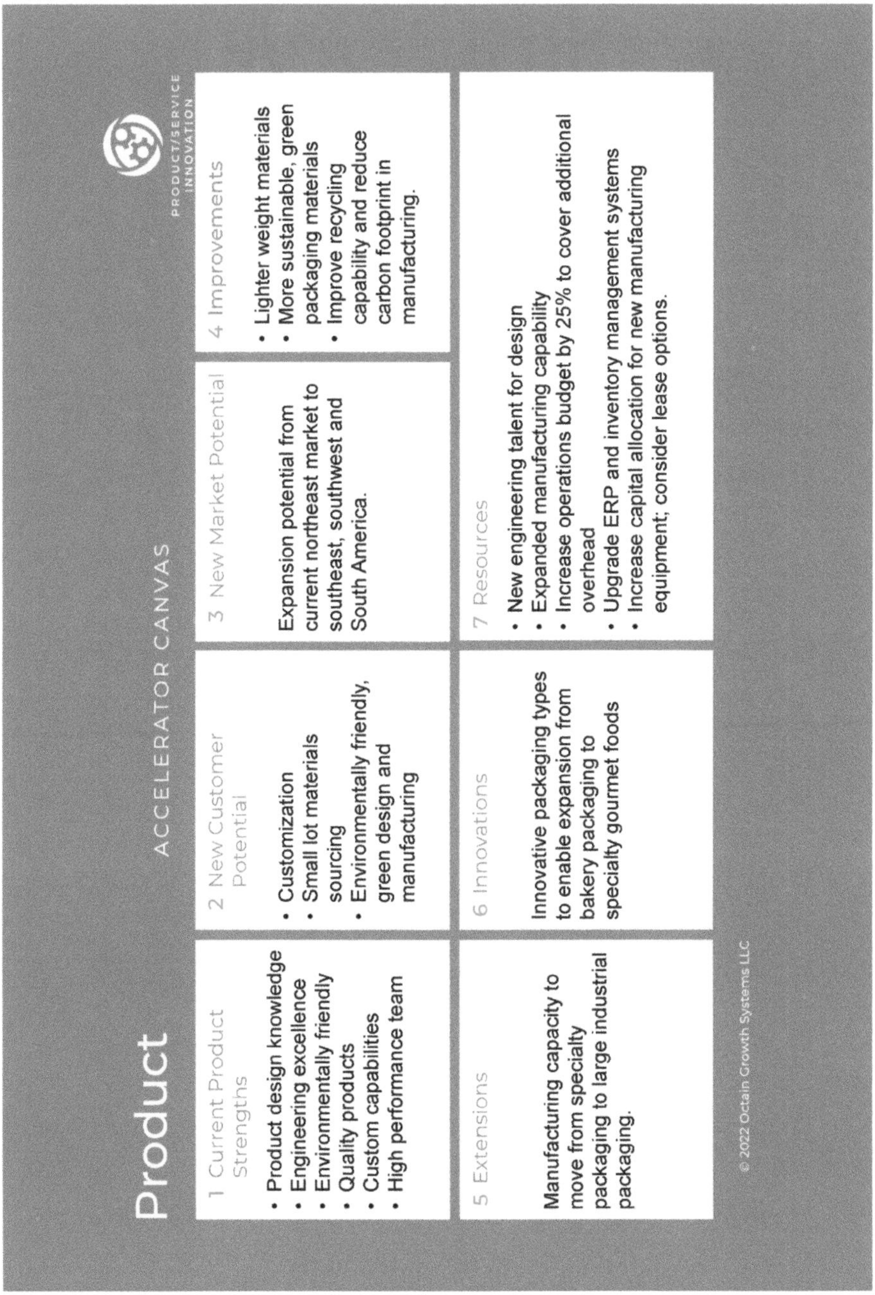
Product
ACCELERATOR CANVAS
PRODUCT/SERVICE INNOVATION
1 Current Product Strengths
• Product design knowledge
• Engineering excellence
• Environmentally friendly
• Quality products
• Custom capabilities
• High performance team
2 New Customer Potential
• Customization
• Small lot materials sourcing
• Environmentally friendly, green design and manufacturing
3 New Market Potential
Expansion potential from current northeast market to southeast, southwest and South America.
4 Improvements
• Lighter weight materials
• More sustainable, green packaging materials
• Improve recycling capability and reduce carbon footprint in manufacturing.
5 Extensions
Manufacturing capacity to move from specialty packaging to large industrial packaging.
6 Innovations
Innovative packaging types to enable expansion from bakery packaging to specialty gourmet foods
7 Resources
• New engineering talent for design
• Expanded manufacturing capability
• Increase operations budget by 25% to cover additional overhead
• Upgrade ERP and inventory management systems
• Increase capital allocation for new manufacturing equipment; consider lease options.
© 2022 Octain Growth Systems LLC

Keys To Product Acceleration

1. Assess your current product strengths to determine the competitive and market strengths of your product or services. Consider how you can use these strengths to compete better in today's digital economy.
2. Set up a team meeting or off-site event to focus on discovering new customer potential. It is great to service existing loyal customers and even better to upsell them into more of your products and services. But real accelerated growth comes from finding an entirely new customer group.
3. Set up a team meeting or off-site event to focus on new market potential. How can your product/service strengths be used in a new niche? If, for example, your product has a strong presence in manufacturing, could it also serve the construction industry?
4. Use the mind map tool to discover ways to improve your products and services. Ask the key question: How can you make your product/service easier to use, more affordable, or faster to get customer results?
5. Use the mind map tool to discover ways to extend your products and services. Ask the key question: How can you expand your product/service capabilities or customer reach?
6. Use the mind map tool to discover ways to innovate your products and services. Ask the key question: What can you do to push the boundaries of your current product/service focus and limitations?
7. Map out the resources you will need in time, talent, money, systems, and tools to accomplish these new product/service goals.

ACTION: Use the example Product Accelerator Canvas in the appendix as a guide to summarize all of your ideas, insights, and decisions on the Product Accelerator Canvas.

You can find more tools and resources for the canvas in the OGS Product Accelerator Canvas on our website at www.octaingrowth.com.

PART III:

GETTING THERE

Chapter 9
SMART EXECUTION

Executives say they lose 40 percent of their strategy's potential value to breakdowns in execution.—Michael Mankins, Harvard Business Review[28]

PLANNING CAN BE a real pain for high-performing business owners, especially when you are on a roll and really want to keep the momentum going. Equally, it's a problem for crisis managers who are so deep in the alligator pit they know if they stop moving to plan they will be devoured.

The purpose of smart execution is to make planning easy *and* turn it from an exercise into a process.

Smart execution is the *process* of getting from where you are today to where you want to be. Smart execution will get you to your destination and goals. Despite that, or maybe because of it, smart execution is a journey.

When you think of the classic hero's journey of good storytelling, it always begins with a life-changing event. Something happens that forces the hero to start a journey to a different place. Along the way, they learn something about themselves they didn't know before. The journey has changed the hero. They will never be the same. They will think and act differently.

You will take your business on a hero's journey when you engage in smart execution. Like the hero of classic fiction, when you follow the path of smart execution, your business will never be the same.

Tri Tool Journeys To New Market Opportunities

Since 1972, Tri Tool has delivered on the winning combination of precision, performance, and people: precision engineering; proven performance and innovation; and people who will always find a way to solve a customer's problem, no matter how challenging. That's Building Performance: The Tri Tool Way.

Tri Tool was at a crossroads in its market position. Market dynamics were changing, especially in its traditional market areas of nuclear energy, oil and gas production, and power generation. The company was eager to explore new market opportunities for its portable machine and welding tools as well as position itself more effectively against competitors in a consolidating market space where smaller competitors were being acquired by global conglomerates.

The company needed assistance in focusing its marketing and sales efforts in four key areas:

1. Global Competitive Landscape—Identify Tri Tool competition within various US and international markets and evaluate the marketing and sales strategies Tri Tool needed to win.
2. Product and Services—Provide sales and distribution partners with a detailed competitive comparison.
3. Market Environment—Determine opportunities and threats in key markets.
4. Target Customer Analysis—Prioritize marketing and sales resources for maximum impact.

Employing our smart execution process, Octain's Growth Architect Program for Tri Tool included competitive analysis and insights for twenty vendors; market environment comparisons for eleven global market segments; review of eighteen customer types; and a comprehensive product and services feature/benefit analysis across three product divisions: portable machine tools, welding tools, and services.

Tri Tool's confidence in choosing new market segments for its high-performance machine tools came from the application of Octain's secret sauce: recommendations based on our decision framework.

Smart Execution Delivers Sustainable Growth

Planning isn't what it used to be.

Even before COVID-19 turned the world upside down and tossed everyone's carefully laid plans around like confetti, planning sessions had lost their luster, because all too often plans failed.

It's tempting to do something many management teams have—forget planning and simply set goals and work your butt off to achieve them. According to HBR, 40 percent of executives think the track record on that approach isn't too great either.

The answer isn't to get better at planning; it is to get better at execution. And that doesn't mean simply exerting more effort. That's when execution becomes an exercise—something you grunt and groan your way through, especially if you are out of shape.

A better option—smart execution—has a successful track record going back ten years.

Figure 35: OGS Smart Execution

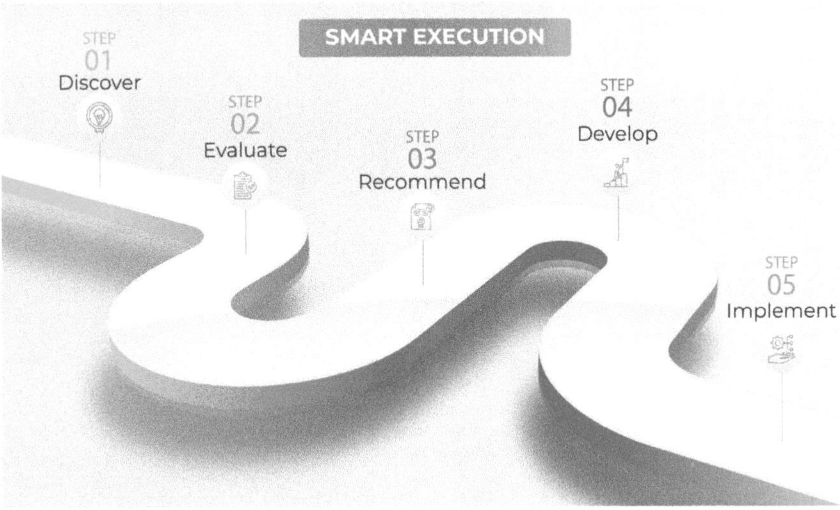

SMART EXECUTION
STEP 01 Discover
STEP 02 Evaluate
STEP 03 Recommend
STEP 04 Develop
STEP 05 Implement

Here are the five steps to smart execution:

1. *Discover*—A combination of assessment and blue-sky thinking that doesn't limit your opportunities to likely outcomes, low-hanging fruit, or incremental growth.
2. *Evaluate*—The process of reviewing the opportunities uncovered in discovery and prioritizing them against goals, resources, and capabilities to choose the one with the highest potential outcomes.
3. *Recommend*—The best way to get things done, using the smart execution decision framework detailed below.
4. *Develop*—The road map for rapid revenue acceleration.
5. *Implement and Automate*—Swing into action with the confidence of a detailed plan.

The really cool thing about smart execution is that it offers a new way to set execution up for success. It is foundational enough to provide structure and elastic enough to provide flexibility.

The first step in smart execution is discovery. You will use discovery to look for new opportunities for your company, products, and services in the year ahead. Don't be satisfied with a little incremental growth; this is all about finding new horizons.

The discovery lens focuses on the six business accelerators covered in detail in chapters three through eight—those that have shown the most sustainable growth over time. As a quick reminder, they are product development, customer acquisition and retention, brand awareness, message clarity, market expansion, and sales and marketing alignment.

The purpose of discovery is to look beyond targeting, which is generally what you see in front of you that typically leads to incremental growth. A typical target is the goal to increase sales by 25 percent next year. Discovery asks more open-ended questions such as, "How can our current product be used to solve a related problem?"

The tools used in discovery are the six accelerator canvases and mind mapping. As a quick reminder they are: brand development, customer acquisition, message clarity, market expansion, sales enablement, and product innovation.

This product/service accelerator canvas from chapter 8 is a reminder that challenges your team to ask those open-ended questions, going beyond simple product improvements to consider innovations, new markets, and new customer potential.

Figure 36: Product/Service Accelerator Canvas

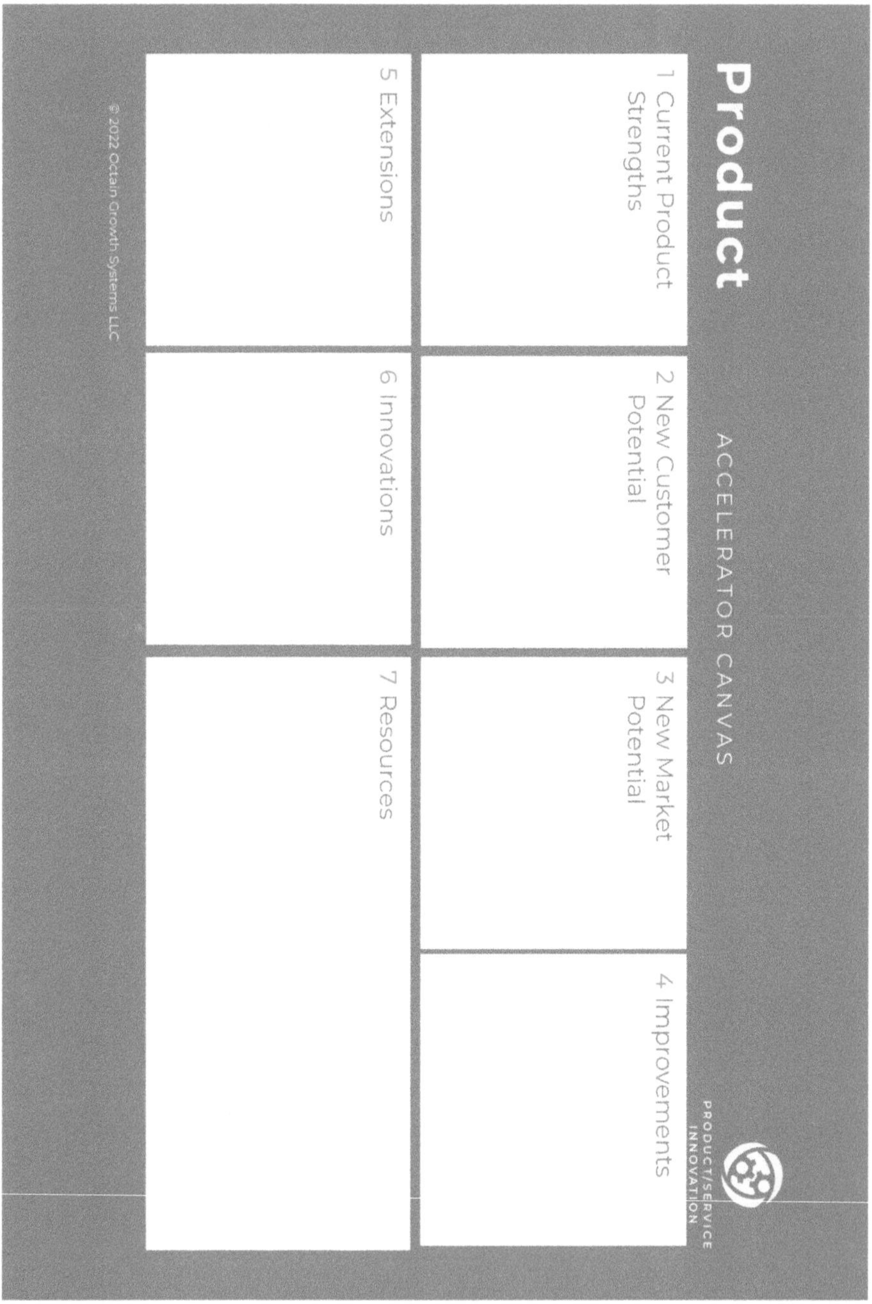
Product
ACCELERATOR CANVAS
1 Current Product Strengths
2 New Customer Potential
3 New Market Potential
4 Improvements
5 Extensions
6 Innovations
7 Resources
PRODUCT/SERVICE INNOVATION
© 2022 Octain Growth Systems LLC

This canvas has three key uses: as a whiteboard to brainstorm new ideas, as an assessment tool to get a snapshot of current capabilities, and as a strategic planning worksheet.

The second step in smart execution is evaluation. Focused evaluation enables your team to choose the best opportunities identified during the discovery process. Evaluation relies on a proven process and well-defined set of criteria designed to take guesswork, silo thinking, turf battles, and knee-jerk responses off the table.

The team needs to start by agreeing on the criteria to be used for the evaluation. Once that has occurred, you can consider various aspects of the proposed opportunity. To evaluate the opportunity for revenue growth and profitability, look at the market and customer opportunities, the competitive advantage it offers, and the resources required for success. Finally, prioritize the opportunity according to revenue potential and likelihood of success within a predefined time-frame, such as twelve months.

Chart 27 shows a typical evaluation grid with a customer example.

Chart 27: Evaluation Grid

Opportunity	TAM/SAM	Competitive Advantage	Upsell Potential	New Customer Potential	New Market Potential	Resources Required	Priority
Describe the opportunity here.	Based on your assessment in discovery, what is the total and salable available market for this opportunity?	Will this opportunity help us compete more or less effectively for new sales?	Does this opportunity enable us to sell more of what we have to existing customers? Volume, related products, etc.	How can this opportunity be used to appeal to more of the same kinds of customers in other areas?	How can this opportunity be used to appeal to different segments or types of customers?	How much/many of our current resources are needed to succeed with this opportunity? What new, not-yet-acquired resources are required?	Each team member ranks the opportunity by priority growth potential and likelihood of success within an established time-frame, e.g., twelve months.
New customer type (segment) identified: hospitality industry.	There are two million customers of this type in our region. We can sell 25 percent of them.	Only one of our five top competitors is targeting this customer segment.	This new customer segment is aligned with our current customer base so may highlight upsell potential.	It is a completely new customer segment.	Selling to these customers opens up the hospitality industry segment to our products.	Talent—new marketing manager required. Marketing—new landing pages, collateral. Budget of $100,000 includes salary.	Assuming five team members, priority ranking might look like this: 1, 6, 3, 7, 2
Opportunity 2							
Opportunity 3							

The third step in smart execution is recommend. Developing recommendations is the secret sauce of smart execution because this is where the process shines.

Your team has done a lot of work so far in discovering and evaluating new opportunities. Now it's time to apply the recommend process so your team has more confidence you are focusing on the right opportunities, and they are providing the anticipated outcome.

Smart Execution Decision Framework

How do you develop your recommendations using smart execution? Here, in a nutshell, is the OGS decision framework:

- Big idea/goal—Quantify your big idea with achievable goals.
- Destination/results—Determine the desired results you are seeking.
- Pathways/journey—Evaluate all the alternate routes to get there.
- Considerations/resources—Consider your current capabilities and the resources required for success.

The Smart Execution Difference

With smart execution, you will build pathways from the goal to the destination—the outcome you want based on understanding the key factors. You will be aware of the considerations that will influence success and can measure their impact *before* starting to implement the solution.

It's a pathway because it is more than just choosing a program; it also involves the implementation and automation to get there.

Let's say you want to generate new leads for your sales team. Also assume this is a new customer segment as detailed in the evaluation grid above. And you know just doing more of what you have always done is not going to cut it. So, which way do you go? You have these strategies to choose from:

- email marketing
- webinars
- social media
- content marketing

All are valid strategies, but which pathway is right for this audience at this time?

You don't want to look at just one pathway. Be prepared to consider several, as many as you can creatively imagine.

Determine The Best Pathway

Use the key considerations worksheet to measure the resources each pathway requires.

Chart 28: Key Considerations Worksheet

Program/ Pathway	TIME	MONEY	TOOLS	TALENT	TIMELINE	MILESTONES	OBSTACLES	PRIORITY

A Simple Formula For Growth

Choosing the right pathway is quite simple when you apply the following formula to each path option: (PR–CR)/TF = GV. That is:

> *Projected revenue – cost of resources expended/time-frame needed to complete = growth value*
>
> Pathway A
> $100,000 – $45,000 (cost of resources) divided by six months = growth value of 9.2
>
> Pathway B
> $500,000 – $135,000 (cost of resources) divided by fourteen months = growth value of 26.1

Of the two pathways to growth explored here, pathway B yields the higher result and should be the top priority for implementation.

The fourth step of smart execution is to develop a road map. Here is where you lay out the pathway for growth. You match the discovery opportunities to the resources required and available so your team has a well-defined road map from start to finish that eliminates trial-and-error decision-making. Like a GPS, know where you are going and exactly how to get there.

Within the OGS, you begin road map–building with the accelerator canvas. Whether you are looking at product development or messaging, your canvas enables your team to take the first step, which is setting the strategy. With your completed canvas, that crucial yet often time-consuming step is done.

The second step is to determine the resource requirements. You did that as you built your pathways to determine which way to go. So with the work already completed, you are almost halfway there.

The third step in the road map process is to set the milestones. Again, that was competed with your pathway development.

The fourth step is to actually build a visual map. Many tools exist to help with that step. For example, you can use a specific product road map tool like Aha!,[29] a social media management tool like Hootsuite,[30] or a general collaboration tool like monday.com.[31]

The fifth step of smart execution is implementation and automation. Automation is your vehicle for driving growth through increasing productivity and improving efficiency. You will want to use cloud-based tools in sales, marketing, productivity, and collaboration that give your team back time, energy, and enthusiasm for the road ahead.

Keys To Smart Execution

1. Discover. A combination of assessment and blue-sky thinking that doesn't limit your opportunities to likely outcomes, low-hanging fruit, or incremental growth.
2. Evaluate. Review the opportunities uncovered in discovery and prioritize against goals, resources, and capabilities to choose the one with the highest potential outcomes.
3. Recommend. The best way to get things done. For this step we use the smart execution decision framework.
4. Develop. The road map for rapid revenue acceleration.
5. Implement and automate. Swing into action with the confidence of a detailed plan.

Chapter 10
IMPLEMENTATION

THE USE OF *automation can have major advantages for SMBs that are facing glaring gaps in IT services that affect their ability to operate at full efficiency and potential.*—Chuck Canton, CEO, Sourcepass

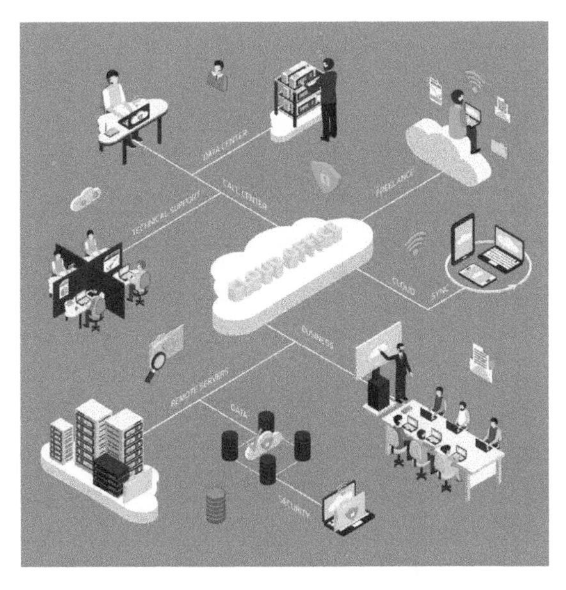

Nor-Cal Controls was growing so rapidly that it was stretching the limits of what its team could do. COVID-19 didn't slow down the company, but the lack of digital tools sure did. Its biggest customer advantage was response time; it was always same day, often within hours. By contrast, its competitors often took days to respond to customer requests.

Nor-Cal was adding new hires at a rapid pace and faced big challenges for onboarding and training due to the pandemic. As a result, its legendary response time slipped badly. Customers started complaining.

Rob Lopez, Nor-Cal's CEO, realized his team had to change the way it was onboarding employees. The Nor-Cal team responded by putting a digital workplace solution in place. Nor-Cal now has an online interviewing, onboarding, and training platform to ensure new and remote employees are fully integrated with the company culture and best practices.

With acceleration through automation, Nor-Cal was able to create new operating efficiencies and recover their reputation as the most responsive, caring, and easiest to work with solar controls company in the industry. Nor-Cal employees returned to exceeding customer expectations with the quality of the company's systems and their customer service.

The decision to invest in automated systems made the difference.

Bring Your Business To The Cloud

Global enterprises have been investing in cloud-based automation for decades. And that investment really showed its value during the COVID-19 pandemic in 2020 and 2021. Because of automation, their employees were able to quickly transition to remote work during the early lockdowns. These large companies were also better positioned for the hybrid work environment that includes at-office and remote workers because they had the automated tools in place.

Small and medium-sized businesses (SMBs) without cloud-based automation in place had to scramble to recover momentum when the lockdowns occurred. The result? Small and medium-sized business owners now have more appreciation for the power of automation to deliver operating efficiencies in their organizations.

In fact, new research from Norwalk, Connecticut-based Xerox indicates that up to 80 percent of organizations believe automation is essential for their survival. The Xerox State and Fate of Small and Medium Business survey[32] conducted by Morning Consult polled 1,200 business decision-makers from companies with twenty-five to one thousand employees in the US, Canada, and the UK.

Among the key findings were:

- 82 percent say digitizing paperwork is important to their survival;
- 75 percent are more reliant on workflow technologies, compared with their pre-pandemic setups;
- 88 percent view security software and hardware that protects business information as core to their longevity, with 75 percent likely to upgrade current solutions this year; and
- 65 percent said remote IT support was a substantial pain point—and 74 percent are likely to invest in better solutions this year.

This is especially true for small and medium-sized marketing departments and consultants, the people the OGS was designed to help.

Put simply, automation has top-line and bottom-line benefits that deliver profits, productivity, and—most importantly—efficiencies for your team, no matter how small it is.

Figure 37 highlights the top benefits that SMBs can realize when they move their business operations to the cloud.

Figure 37: Reduce Costs, Improve Efficiencies

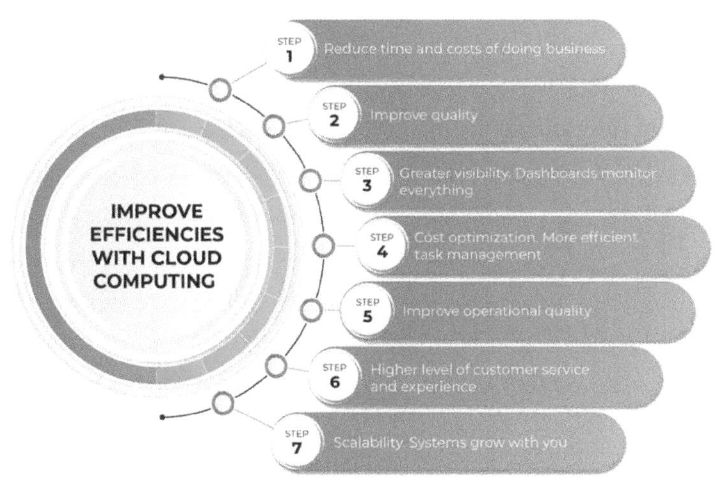

Technology Must-Haves

The power in bringing your business to the cloud occurs from choosing the right systems, technology, and tools. Technology is available today to assist business owners and marketers in every industry to bring all or part of their operations to the cloud.

The good news is the solution you need is almost certainly in the market. If not, dozens of custom software development firms like RoleModel Software in Holly Springs, North Carolina, can design a custom process and system for your organization.

The bad news is the market is crowded with dozens of solutions in every category. Finding the perfect automation fit for your company's needs can be confusing, frustrating, and expensive in terms of time and money.

Help is out there, as there are automation partners across the country that can audit your current infrastructure, help you choose the right systems, and install and maintain them. With an automation partner, bringing your business to the cloud is easier and the ROI payback is faster.

Bringing your business to the cloud involves automating back-end operations (enterprise resource planning systems, inventory management, order management, and purchasing) and front-end customer-facing operations (marketing, sales, customer service, and customer experience).

OGS focuses on the systems, technology, and tools that support the growth accelerators, which include:

- appointment booking
- proposal development
- marketing automation
- sales enablement
- customer service

Professional service firms, especially consultants or anyone who trades time for dollars, can benefit exponentially from moving their operations to the cloud.

Appointment Booking

Bringing your appointment scheduling online frees you from the mundane. It gives customers flexibility and protects your time when you need it. The software noted below is worth a look.

Calendaring software like Calendly[33] and TidyCal[34] are great options for booking individual client appointments.

For a more robust appointment setting solution that includes virtual administrative support for class scheduling and training, try TimeTap[35], which has features for multiple locations, class scheduling, customized booking forms, and automatic payments.

SimplyBook.me[36] is an online booking system for professional services companies that offers online booking, notifications, payments, and marketing incentives like coupons, gift cards, memberships, and product sales. In addition, SimplyBook.me offers listings in its professional services directory.

There is a variety of industry-specific booking software out there too, such as Legwork[37] for doctors and dentists, Mindbody[38] for fitness classes and gyms, and Picktime[39] for hair salons.

Proposal Software

If your company submits proposals for jobs manually, especially in professional services, you should strongly consider investing in proposal software. It will drastically cut the non-billable time you spend developing your proposals and it monitors the prospect's response by tracking when, what, and how they view what you sent them.

Imagine knowing when your prospect read your proposal instead of wondering and sending blind follow-ups.

Imagine knowing what pages caught their attention. Was it benefits? Features? Pricing? Knowing this better equips you to send a follow-up designed to appropriately respond to their specific interests.

That's exactly what proposal software like PandaDoc,[40] Proposify,[41] and Bidsketch[42] can do for you. Most offer a limited free version or trial.

You may also want to check out the top twelve proposal software options noted in a HubSpot blog post[43] written in 2018 and updated in 2022.

Email Marketing Systems

If your primary marketing efforts are built around email marketing, you can find many effective and inexpensive solutions on the market today.

The top ten email marketing systems as ranked by *PC Magazine*[44] are:

1. Salesforce Pardot
2. Campaigner
3. HubSpot
4. Mailchimp
5. Sendinblue
6. GetResponse
7. Keap
8. Zoho Campaigns
9. Campaign Monitor
10. Constant Contact

Marketing Automation

Marketing automation software automates many baseline marketing functions that enable your team to excel at demand and lead generation. Options run from email marketing systems to sophisticated demand and lead generation and prospecting platforms.

Marketing automation is a critical success component of digital and social media marketing. Based on extensive research for my clients, my six top choices for marketing automation are noted in chart 29.

Chart 29: Best-In-Class Marketing Automation Systems

Product	Pros	Cons	Pricing
ActiveCampaign	Robust suite of tools built around email marketing. Easy to design templates. Lots of custom features in professional package.	Number of options can be confusing. Price rises quickly with size of contact list.	$9 to $229 per month for 500 contacts to $69 to $359 per month for 5,000 contacts
Autopilot	Clever, visually intuitive design canvas for email automation, lead nurturing, and reporting.	No integrated CRM. Built around email marketing.	$49 to $249 per month
Keap (formerly Infusionsoft)	One-stop-shop email, marketing automation, CRM platform. Large breadth of features, flexibility.	Complex; longer learning curve than others.	$79 to $199 per month
HubSpot	Granddaddy of inbound marketing platforms. Robust feature set focuses on lead capture and conversion.	Complexity; high learning curve; expensive. No real marketing automation in starter level.	$40 to $3,200 per month
SharpSpring	Solid small business marketing solution. Good social management and analytics options.	Expensive for businesses with small contact lists.	$550 per month for 1,500 contacts to $1,250 per month for 20,000 contacts
Ontraport	Powerful email, marketing automation, and CRM solution. Easy to set up. Great customer support.	Flexibility can lead to complexity and confusion.	$79 to $497 per month

Sales Enablement (CRM)

A robust customer relationship management (CRM) tool is one cloud sales enablement tool no business should be without. CRM software solutions are all about building customer relationships. They enable your sales team to connect with prospects and track their activity with your business from first connection to close of sale.

CRM systems include contact management, lead management, opportunity management, and sales forecasting. Some integrate with marketing automation systems—theirs and others.

Five top picks for CRM, based on what worked best for my clients, are noted in chart 30.

Chart 30: Best-In-Class SMB CRM Software Solutions

Product	Pros	Cons	Pricing
Salesforce Sales Cloud	The leader in CRM. Good opportunity management and extensive reporting. Integrates with Salesforce marketing and service clouds.	Overkill in features and pricing for smaller businesses. Very limited essentials starter offering.	$25 to $300 per user per month; $75 professional edition most value for small businesses
Nutshell	Agile, easy-to-use CRM with fast learning curve. Includes all basic CRM functions.	Limited starter level sales automation. Weak mobile app. Steep price climb after starter level.	$19 to $35 per user per month
Copper	Easy-to-use CRM for small businesses that offers key CRM functions at a competitive price. Nice integration with G Suite.	Limited workflow automation. Cannot disburse leads automatically based on tracked conversion rates.	$24 to $119 per user per month
Pipedrive	CRM more focused on deal flow than contact management. Great lead tracking from multiple channels.	Maximum of 1,000 names on an email send. Needs better multichannel marketing features.	$15 to $59 per user per month
Zoho CRM	Part of the extensive Zoho small business suite, comprehensive easy-to-use CRM solution. Customizable. Great analytics for tracking.	Older user interface. Features can be limited on lower-priced tiers.	$12 to $100 per user per month

Customer Service

To meet customer expectations in today's digital marketplace, you need to keep customers happy by delivering a seamless customer experience (CX) to every customer. They expect support through a range of channels and devices as quickly as possible. Customers now demand an Amazon-like experience from every supplier, as noted in a 2021 blog post from SuperOffice.[45]

Figure 38: Most Important Attribute Of The Customer Experience

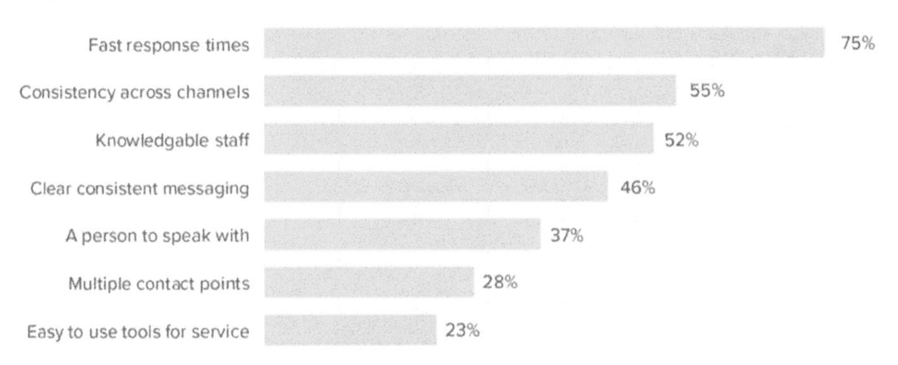

Phone and email support alone just don't cut it anymore given today's challenging times. Any small business owner can radically change their customer service experience with two online CX investments: apps and live chat.

I've Got An App For That

If the COVID-19 lockdowns of 2020 and 2021 had occurred ten years earlier, daily life would have been nearly impossible. But since apps now exist for just about everything, from online groceries to distance learning and Teladocs, things did not come to a standstill during that challenging time.

Apps can be a real advantage for SMBs in markets with much larger, better-funded competitors. Millennial and Gen-Z customers simply expect to do business with you through an app.

A well-designed app lets your customers place orders, check shipment status, log trouble tickets, and more.

App developers are plentiful and global with a wide range of pricing and experience. Chart 31 provides some key considerations for choosing an app developer. Use this checklist as your interview guide and rank candidates on their ability to meet your project's needs.

Chart 31: Considerations For Choosing An App Developer

Capability	Expertise	Rating (1 to 5)
Design Experience: understands design and utility and how your customer interacts with apps.	Five to ten years of experience	
Business Focus	Understands your business needs and how an app can best support them.	
Relationship Driven	Will work with you over the long term through an extended product lifecycle.	
Client References	Provide at least three recent client references.	
Price	Be willing to pay for what you really need to support your customers over the long term.	

Discover Live Chat

Another great customer experience automation system to invest in is live chat. Live chat changes your website from a static information site to a live customer resource center. Research from SuperOffice[46] shows that companies can lower response times from hours to seconds with live chat as show in Chart 32.

Chart 32: Customer Service Response Times With Live Chat

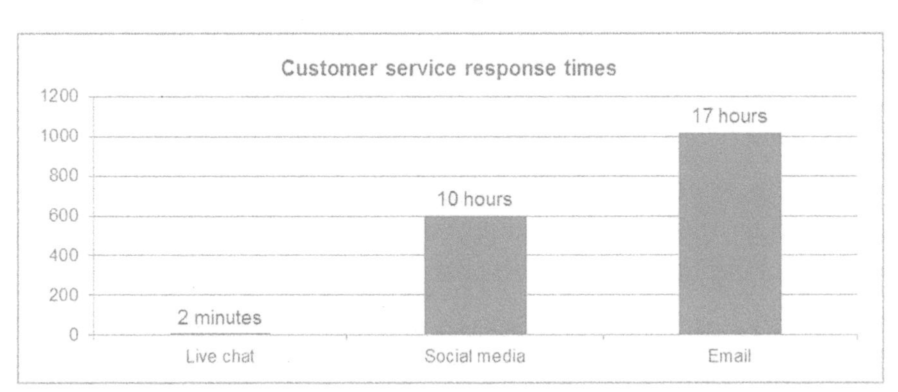

Most importantly, live chat helps you increase sales. The American Marketing Association found that B2B companies that used live chat saw, on average, a 20 percent increase in conversions and customers who chat are three times more likely to buy.[47]

The three live chat software solutions you may want to consider are LiveChat,[48] Zendesk,[49] and Olark.[50]

Keys To Acceleration Through Automation

Transitioning your business operations from manual or on-premises systems to cloud-based solutions can be daunting. Automation requires rethinking what and how you do your day-to-day operational projects and tasks.

However, long-term success in the remote economy requires rethinking and reinvention. And it's worth it. When you transition to the cloud, you get operational efficiencies, flexibility, and adaptability to the changing economic times—whatever comes down the road.

1. Map out the costs and resources of your current solution versus the costs and resources needed by a cloud solution.
2. Evaluate and determine what functions should be automated and in what order.
3. Prepare for a phased approach to automating functions to minimize business disruption.
4. Research the availability and viability of a cloud solution for your business.
5. Talk to peers who have made the transition to gauge the benefit and impact on your business. Have detailed discussions with potential vendors.
6. Engage an automation partner to assess your needs and develop a set of recommendations and a blueprint for transition.
7. Create a set of KPIs to measure the success of your transition.
8. Assign IT, marketing, sales, and service personnel to work directly with your automation partner to develop, implement, roll out, and train all staff on the new automation.
9. Measure the success of the automation to ensure increased efficiency of operations.
10. Adjust systems and processes as needed during initial implementation to achieve maximum benefit.

Chapter 11

THE HUMAN ELEMENT: PUTTING PEOPLE FIRST

A successful person finds the right place for himself. A successful leader finds the right place for others.—John C. Maxwell

YOU CAN HAVE it all: the technology, the tools, the process. But if you don't have the right people in the right roles with the right attitudes and capacities, none of that matters.

When speaking to CEO groups like Vistage about accelerated growth, the number one reason CEOs give me for growth challenges is people. And it is getting worse. The Great Resignation of 2020–2021 that saw people quitting their jobs in large numbers is continuing in 2022. People need a better reason to work than a paycheck.

According to the US Bureau of Labor Statistics,[51] four million Americans quit their jobs in July 2021. Resignations peaked in April 2021 and remained abnormally high for several months, with a record-breaking 10.9 million open jobs at the end of July 2021.

Employees thirty to forty-five years old have had the greatest increase in resignation rates, with an average increase of more than 20 percent between 2020 and 2021.

A study by the *Harvard Business Review*[52] found these midcareer employees were resigning because the pressures of their jobs combined with the pandemic caused them to rethink their work and life goals.

The bottom line: People are your most important asset. Whatever you do to implement the growth strategies presented so far, it starts with putting people first.

CEOs nod when they hear this. Of course, they say. We know. The question is how, especially given how rapidly the global workforce is shifting. Leadership and management styles that worked ten years ago or even two years ago no longer apply, as the Great Resignation clearly shows.

It's time to rethink leadership and management for a post-pandemic, remote-first work environment. Some human resource areas of focus that have helped our clients use OGS to its maximum potential are:

- bridging personalities and teamwork
- rightsizing roles—fitting roles to people
- boosting team performance with workflows to take advantage of automation

Bridging Personalities And Teamwork

The personality test is a staple of the HR department. You can take your pick of the DiSC profile, Myers-Briggs, Strengths Finder, HEXACO, and many more.

My personal favorite is the Enneagram model, for two reasons:

- The nine types of the Enneagram model provide a better understanding of personality and work style than the four to six typical with many other approaches.
- The Enneagram model shows how to use the Enneagram personality types to develop higher performing teams as shown in Figure 39.

This is because the Enneagram model explains personality types *and* shows how each type is instrumental in problem-solving, according to Matt Schlegel, author of the book, *Teamwork 9.0: Successful Workgroup Problem Solving Using the Enneagram.*[53]

"Using the Enneagram as a framework for solving problems highlights how each Enneagram type is attuned to a particular step in the problem-solving process. It seems that humans instinctively know how to solve problems as a team and the Enneagram describes that methodology," Schlegel said.

Figure 39: Enneagram Problem-Solving Methods

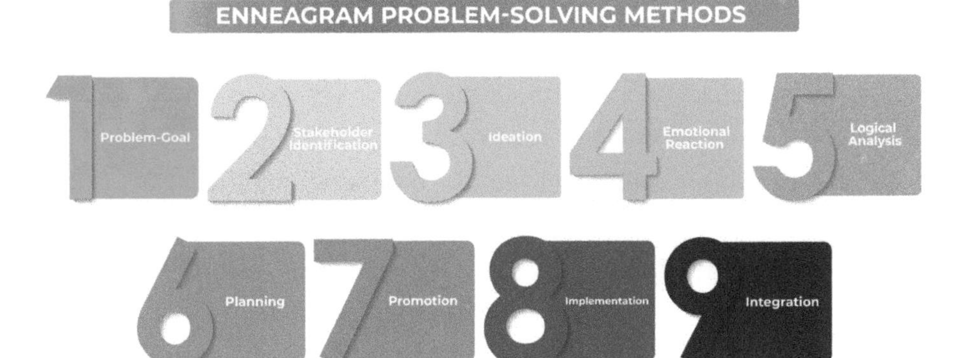

Each of the steps relates directly to the strongest energy of each of the Enneagram types, noted in figure 40.

Figure 40: The Enneagram Model

The magic is in how well they fit and work together. Schlegel explains it this way in his book:[54]

- Type 1—Reformers excel at problem identification.
- Type 2—Helpers are instinctively committed to teams, bringing together stakeholders "committed to solving the problem and realizing the vision of a beautiful world."
- Type 3—Achievers excel at ideation because they are wired to consider all ideas without the emotional prejudging that affects other personality types.
- Type 4—Individualists begin the process of qualification of an idea because of their quick emotional reaction to ideas.
- Type 5—Investigators continue the process of qualification with their tendency toward collecting information and logical analysis of a problem's pros and cons.
- Type 6—Loyalists excel at the planning stage because they are always looking to reduce uncertainty, anxiety, and risk. With them leading the charge, your team will find the best path to the goal.

- Type 7—Enthusiasts are the promoters of the group. You can count on these personality types to help everyone on the team get excited about the plan that has been proposed.
- Type 8—Challengers excel at implementation. They are done with the talk and the cheerleading and want to get into the action and execute the plan.
- Type 9—Peacemakers help smooth the path for execution by using their gifts of empathy and calm understanding to reduce anxiety. They soothe concerns about the changes that are taking place in the organization as it implements the plan.

As your team moves forward with smart execution and automation, the Enneagram model of personalities and problem-solving can be a real asset.

Rightsizing Roles

The team is in disarray. Everyone from the CEO to the head of customer service has the same complaint: "We're over budget. We didn't hit our deadline. We have to go back to the drawing board." Sound familiar? That's usually when The People Catalysts gets the call.

To change that dynamic, The People Catalysts' trainers start with an assessment to determine each person's core nature: mover, shaker, prover, or maker, so each person can better understand why they do things a certain way.

"People adopt the new information when everybody on the team gets to lead. But everybody leads at different times and in a different way. Only 15 percent of the population will say yes to a new idea. Shakers are the 25 percent who say no if it wasn't their idea and 35 percent of the population are provers who say no because it isn't going to work. And 25 percent of the population of makers, say, 'Hey guys, I just got done cleaning this place from the last time you messed it up.' Innovation is painful for them," explained Karla Nelson, CEO of The People Catalysts.

"It removes the resistance when I just say, 'I'm going to understand who you are at your core, and I'm going to help you focus. We'll identify the parts of the work that you do well and let everybody else do the parts of the work that they do well.' When you do that, you encouraged the brilliance in somebody," Nelson added.

Peak performance from high-achieving teams is the goal of every corporate leader, especially today. As the nature of work continues its fluid remote evolution, leaders and employees are both feeling the whiplash of changing workplace dynamics: is it okay at home or is it time to return to the office?

That uncertainty is compounded by the corporate need for revenue and profit recovery to regain market and operational ground lost during the height of the pandemic response. For many organizations, revenue recovery means making difficult talent assessments and decisions. Holding onto your most valuable employees requires a deep understanding of your people, their capabilities, and how to incentivize peak performance.

With all tools and effort put into hiring, it might surprise you to learn that traditional management has designed jobs so only 1 percent of the people can do the whole job well. That's exactly what the team at The People Catalysts discovered when they took an in-depth look at corporate work environments in businesses that were in the process of being sold and needed to maximize talent value.

While the 1 percent may be happy, the other 99 percent of your employees suffer through WeakWork, which is slow, boring, and miserable, and then zoom through PeakWork, which is fast and fun. After they are done with their PeakWork, they have nothing left for the rest of the day, except WeakWork.

The People Catalysts' studies reveal that most companies approach talent management in the twenty-first century with the twentieth century work style. Hiring is done by who best fits the job description and whatever management hierarchy and company culture has evolved rather than finding the best person and creating the job for them.

"The truth is it's much more powerful to have the work fit the people than have the people fit the work," said Nelson.

That realization led to the discovery of a unique talent assessment methodology The People Catalysts has branded the Who-Do Method.[55]

Reshaping Roles To Fit People

As noted above, the Who-Do Method identifies four core natures of work: mover, shaker, prover, and maker. According to Nelson:

Movers are early adopters who are natural doers. They know how to get and keep things moving. These people easily plan how things will get done, choose the best idea, and introduce the right people to each other. Movers are the "fast forward" on a remote control.

Shakers are early adopters who are natural thinkers. They like to shake things up with new ideas and easily solve problems by seeing the larger context of a situation. Some of their ideas may seem outlandish, but many are potential home runs. Shakers are the "power" button on a remote control.

Provers are later adopters who are natural thinkers. Often seen as skeptics by others, they challenge new ideas. Comfortable with proven solutions, these people feel like it's their duty to warn others about what can go wrong. Provers like to "rewind" things and go through them again.

Makers are later adopters who are natural doers. As great finishers, they put ideas into action, dotting the i's and crossing the t's. Makers honor the details that others miss and would rather do "real" work than sit in meetings. Makers are the "play" button.

These core natures explain how people will react to new ideas, how they excel in their roles, and—most importantly—how they contribute to the team's peak performance.

"The reason why we called our core natures movers, shakers, provers, and makers is because everybody always says the 'movers and shakers' of the world. Yeah, that's great. But we need everybody. We just need them at different times. Too often the movers and shakers get all the glory in the world. But if you don't have that prover or maker person to hand off to, that project is not going to get done," explained Nelson.

"Too often people are criticized just for who they are. Like when people say, 'I can't stand dealing with a Debbie Downer.' Instead of focusing on that, why not let them poke every single hole they could ever think of. And they just light up, beaming because that's what they do," she added.

This worked for a national transportation company whose management team had been fighting over the implementation of a safety standard for two years. Without it, they were out of business. Using the Who-Do Method, the engineers were able to eliminate the arguing and replace it with a conscious effort to discover the flaws in the best idea. That freed them to creatively eliminate those flaws. After two years of failure, the team was able to agree on a safety standard in one hour.

Learn more about The People Catalysts on its website.[56]

Boost Team Performance By Matching Collaboration Tools To Workflows

Just as it takes having the right people and personalities in the right roles to achieve smart execution, it also takes the right tools.

No tool set is more important at this stage than collaboration tools that improve workflows.

Collaboration tools are meant to increase team productivity. To do that, they need to be widely used across the team and become integrated into the team's day-to-day operations. That seems to be a given. So it might surprise you to learn that collaboration systems and tools meant to enhance productivity might actually deter it. That happens when tools are not matched to the intrinsic or predetermined way a particular team works together—its workflow dynamic.

The Workflow Dynamic

How well a team uses various collaboration tools like project management, messaging, and communication software depends in part on how well that tool is suited to the team's workflow process and working style. For example, a marketing team that is engaged in real-time, fast-paced collaboration on a campaign that includes content, design, analytics, and audience sentiment analysis requires different tools from an IT maintenance team whose collaboration consists primarily of different people with different expertise, each doing their part and bringing it all together as a finished product.

Collaboration Platform Hierarchy

It might help the matching process to visualize your collaboration tool options as a hierarchy with the primary office suite options (Google and Microsoft) as the foundation. They offer all-in-one solutions for project management as a productivity core and messaging/videoconferencing solutions as a communication core. Those can be used in addition to the office suite options, depending on your team's working style or preference.

The major office suites include features for chat and collaboration that may suffice for simple workflows. However, large teams, geographically dispersed teams, and complex workflows usually require tools with features specific to their needs. Twist by Doist, for example, is designed to support geographically dispersed teams. There are benefits to each layer of the hierarchy depending on your team's needs.

Barry runs a ten-person product development team for a large plastics manufacturer. The team operates around its six-month rolling product road map, which includes feature requests from engineering, sales, marketing, and customer service. His company has standardized on Microsoft 365, with Microsoft Teams for communication and chat. His team can use an all-in-one project manager like Basecamp or Asana, for example, and probably make it work. But his team will be more productive with collaboration software designed specifically for product road maps such as Roadmap Planner or Productboard.

Lakeisha is the marketing director at a fast-paced consumer products brand in Chicago. Her twenty-two-member team includes web designers in San Francisco, content developers in Atlanta, social media marketers in India, and digital advertising specialists in London. Her company uses Microsoft 365 and G Suite and so does her marketing group. Lakeisha needs a collaboration solution for a geographically spread team that supports Microsoft and Google applications. She might choose Monday.com for collaboration and the messaging app Twist for communication.

Figure 41: Collaboration Platform Hierarchy*

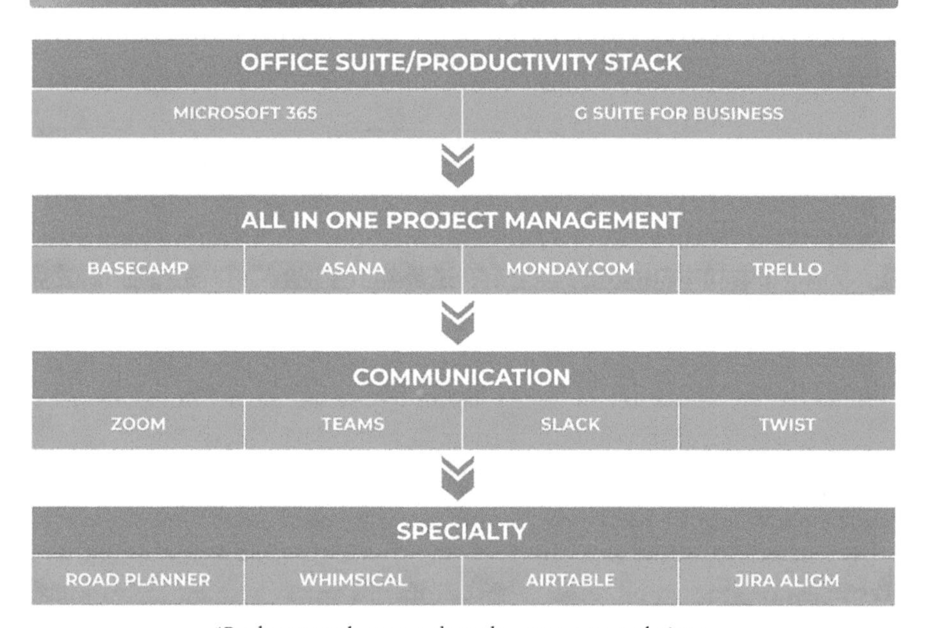

*Products noted as examples only, not recommendations.

Stepping Through The Matching Process

There are a number of actions your organization can take to match team workflows with the collaboration software that will work best for them.

- *Know your team's workflow.* The key questions to determine are:
  - Does your team have a documented workflow or is it an ad hoc collection of tasks? A documented workflow will enable you to determine the best team-tools match.
  - Are member roles and responsibilities included in the workflow or is it simply based on functions? Including

roles and responsibilities in your workflow increases the viability of your team-workflow match. It also helps team members effectively use the workflow.

- Is your workflow being followed? Workflows don't benefit the organization if they are ignored by team members. If yours are not being used, get the team together for an honest discussion of why. Workflows, like any process, can get outdated as things change. And we know things are changing fast now. An open discussion, followed by revisions, will make your workflows vital again.

- *Determine your function/feature short list.* An evaluation of your workflow will highlight the features and functions most needed by your team. Prioritize them into three buckets: must-have, good to have, and nice to have. Nice to haves are features your team can easily live without. Once that list is complete, do a solution check. Go beyond the marketing-speak on the product company website. Check evaluation sites like Capterra and user reviews. For a full department or enterprise solution, make sure to get a live demo.
- *Focus on remote teams first.* In the past, companies typically purchased systems for the office workers and then rolled them out to remote workers when and if they had them. Today, the opposite is true. Your first consideration should be the needs of your remote teams, then collaboration between hybrid workplaces of in-office and remote teams.
- *Evaluate the tools you use today.* How are they working? Have certain teams or team members become attached to specific products? Learn why and discover if that attachment is a benefit or detriment to overall team productivity.
- *Determine integration capabilities.* Some tools have broader integration capabilities than others. Determine your organization's minimum requirements and make sure they are met.

- *Have a process for approving new software.* Make sure that process is known and followed. This will reduce the likelihood of teams purchasing their own solution, which with cloud computing is very easy to do, especially when the team is remote and/or geographically dispersed.
- *Publish a directory of collaboration tools on the corporate intranet.* Go beyond the list of "approved" tools and capture which teams are using what tools, how long they have had them (good indicator of value), and how often they switch tools (warning sign of a dysfunctional team). Enable reviews, feedback, and suggestions for new tools in the database to capture tribal knowledge.

You have a wider selection of collaboration, messaging, and communication tools available than ever before. The good news is there are tools to effectively support all your different and diverse teams' workflows. Start by understanding your teams' workflow dynamics, and then choose tools that work best for them across all levels of the collaboration hierarchy. That's the simple formula for effective remote workplace collaboration.

Keys To Putting People First:

1. Invest significant time in getting to know who your people are, what they love to do, and the type of work that will enable them to thrive.
2. The Enneagram model, which matches personality to problem-solving skills, can be a great asset to improving personal and team productivity.
3. A great guide to personalities and problem-solving is available in Matt Schlegel's book on teamwork.
4. A great guide to matching people to their best job roles can be found from The People Catalysts.

5. Boost team performance and help people perform at their best by providing them with the right tools for collaboration.

6. How well a team uses various collaboration tools like project management, messaging, and communication software depends in part on how well each tool is suited to the team's workflow process and working style. Take the time to match tools to workflows and see productivity skyrocket.

Chapter 12
LEADERSHIP: LEADING THE CHANGE

The goal of many leaders is to get people to think more highly of the leader. The goal of a great leader is to help people to think more highly of themselves.—J. Carla Northcutt, educator and theologian

What kind of leader are you? And more importantly, what kind of leader do your people need today? Gone, hopefully forever, are the authoritarian dinosaurs of the old-school workplace.

Today's millennial and Gen Z employees respond best to leadership styles that are welcoming and open. Two styles that have been effective are participative leadership and servant leadership.

Participative Leadership

"Participative leadership is a style of leadership in which all members of the organization work together to make decisions. Participative leadership is also known as democratic leadership, as everyone is encouraged to participate," said career company Indeed[57].

In participative leadership, the leader is a facilitator to group discussion and decision, not the arbitrator. The group discusses, decides, and acts in agreement.

"Participative leadership is most successful in organizations or companies that have defined roles requiring little management or oversight, like universities, technology companies, or construction firms," said Indeed.

However, along with some structure agreed upon in advance and an understanding of the personality and problem-solving skills of the Enneagram model, just about any organization can benefit from some form of participative leadership.

Servant Leadership

A widely used term today, the concept of servant leadership is attributed to Robert K. Greenleaf, who used the phrase in "The Servant as Leader," an essay he first published in 1970. In it, Greenleaf said:

> *The servant-leader is servant first... It begins with the natural feeling that one wants to serve, to serve first. Then conscious choice brings one to aspire to lead. That person is sharply different from one who is leader first, perhaps because of the need to assuage an unusual power drive or to acquire material possessions...The leader-first and the servant-first are two extreme types. Between them there are shadings and blends that are part of the infinite variety of human nature.*
>
> *The difference manifests itself in the care taken by the servant-first leader to make sure that other people's highest priority needs are being served. The best test, and difficult to administer, is: Do those served grow as persons? Do they, while being served, become healthier, wiser, freer, more autonomous, more likely themselves to become servants?*

Aspiring to the goal of a servant leader is one thing; making the transition, especially for old-school directive leaders, is another. One of the best resources available for making a transformative change is Ken Blanchard's book, *The Servant Leader*.[58] Another is John C. Maxwell's 1998 book, *The 21 Irrefutable Laws of Leadership: Follow Them and People Will Follow You*.[59]

Communication Is Key

Transforming your leadership style is only half the equation for leaders in today's dynamically changing workplace environment. The other critical factor of leading transformative change in your organization is connected communications. This is a need the remote work revolution has amplified, explained Kimberly Layne, author of *Connections Change Everything*.[60]

"Leadership before was really tactical on the project, on the sales goal, on the revenue goal. It's still about that, but the way for leaders to really succeed is to have a pulse on your people: how they're doing emotionally, being empathetic to their situation, understanding some of the challenges that they're facing," Layne said.

Sadly, too many leadership communications are disconnected and fragmented. And the digital world we all live in today is partially to blame. "It's only getting worse with our virtual work environment and the increased use of social media and digital technology to get stuff done. We have to be selective as leaders, educating ourselves and our teams as to when it's appropriate to use digital technology and when it's better to use a human connection like picking up the phone and speaking directly to the person," Layne explained.

Connected communication starts with the affirmation and collaboration that comes from practicing good listening skills. As Layne puts it, "mastering the soft stuff that makes the hard stuff work. Meaning if you don't have empathy and an emotional relationship and connection with your people, you're not going to get the hard stuff. They're not going to fight for you if you're not invested in them.

"Your role as a leader is to recreate emotion in your relationships because people are motivated by emotion," she continued. "People buy on emotion.

People are willing to work harder based on emotion. Your job is to build your emotional connections with your people to get business results."

Today's digital workplace continues to evolve with a change rate that shows no sign of slowing down. These two skills—teamwork by understanding team personality dynamics and connected communications—will help strengthen your digital leadership skills.

Stepping Forward Into OGS

Making the commitment to step into a new growth system is a big one. It means change at every level of the organization from leadership to employees and out into your organizational network of partners, vendors, and consultants.

Since 2004, hundreds of CEOs and marketers in industries as diverse as apparel to trucking have made the leap to OGS and attained accelerated growth in profits, productivity, and efficiency, with an average revenue increase of 33 percent in twelve to eighteen months.

Start Here And Now

Finished the book and ready to put everything you have learned into action? Here are the ten steps we use to start clients on the road to growth transformation with OGS.

1. Plan a Discovery Day. This is a mash-up of an off-site event and an executive retreat. Book a day or weekend away from the office and bring in all your remote managers and key contributors.
2. Use the six OGS accelerator canvases as a whiteboard to capture information on what your team knows and is doing today. For the first run-through of each of the canvases, make it a high-level brainstorming session. Use the same order as the book to capture this collective wisdom.
    a. Brand Development
    b. Customer Acquisition
    c. Messaging Clarity
    d. Market Expansion
    e. Sales Enablement
    f. Product/Service Innovation
3. Do a gap analysis. Evaluate the information collected on these canvases. Where are you strongest, weakest? Where do you have too much focus? Where is there not enough? What's missing? What is under- or over-resourced?
4. Get ready to start the smart execution planning process by prioritizing your focus on the canvas(es) that:
    a. Have the most holes, least resources, and need the most support.
    b. Show the most growth potential using the formula found in chapter 9.
5. Rank the canvases for implementation from one to six based on these priorities.

6. Assign planning teams to each canvas by priority depending on resources available.
7. Book a planning review session thirty days out for a review of each team's work with their canvas.
8. Review progress in thirty days with the expectation that each team will have recommendations for smart execution and automation of their canvas.
9. Approve the canvases by priority according to opportunity and resources.
10. Assign implementers, set metrics for completion, and go.

APPENDIX

Brand

ACCELERATOR CANVAS

BRAND DEVELOPMENT

1 Brand Values	2 Brand Promise	3 Tagline	4 Brand Personality
5 Brand Voice	6 Logo	7 Visual Brand	

Customer

ACCELERATOR CANVAS

CUSTOMER ACQUISITION

1 Demographics, Psychographics

2 Needs, Wants, Desires

3 Values & Motivations

4 Buying Patterns

5 Decision Influencers

6 Social Connections

7 Customer Persona Profile

Message

ACCELERATOR CANVAS

1 THE BIG IDEA

2 Core Message

3 Positioning Statement

4 Supporting Messages

5 Benefits

6 Features

7 Results

MESSAGE CLARITY

Marketing

ACCELERATOR CANVAS

MARKET EXPANSION

1 Goals	2 Approach	3 Marketing Strategies	4 Marketing Tactics
5 Channels	6 Success Metrics	7 Resources	

Sales

ACCELERATOR CANVAS

SALES ENABLEMENT

1 Sales Enablement Team Profile	2 Sales & Marketing Team Alignment Strategies	3 Marketing Enablement Strategies	4 Sales Process
5 Systems, tools and technologies	6 Success Metrics	7 Resources	

Product ACCELERATOR CANVAS

PRODUCT/SERVICE INNOVATION

1 Current Product Strengths	2 New Customer Potential	3 New Market Potential	4 Improvements
5 Extensions	6 Innovations	7 Resources	

ACKNOWLEDGMENTS

Growth isn't possible without the family, friends, peers, and colleagues who support, encourage, nudge, and sometimes even admonish you along the way. That's true for life and especially true for this book.

To my wonderful clients and coaches, who over the last ten years have helped and challenged me to keep developing, evolving, and reinventing the OGS, especially Steve Pappas, Laurie Earl, Steve Simonetto, Frank Denning, Michelle Stofan, Jeff Briggs, and Kevin McGrew.

To my mentors and friends for their wisdom, advice, and encouragement over the many ups and downs of bringing the OGS to life, especially Deb Brown Maher, Ray Bryant, Christine Crandall, and Kelle Santin, my personal trainer who kept my energy up for those long days of writing.

To my mom, Mary E. Fleig; my sister, Catherine Nadel; and my cousin, Mary Grider, for always being there.

To my writing, editing, and design team at Indie Books International Henry DeVries, Devin DeVries, Adrienne Moch, Gail Sevrens, Lisa Lucas, and Steve Plummer.

Most importantly, to my Lord and Savior, Jesus Christ, for everything I have to offer to my readers and the world.

Acts 17:28: For in him we live, and move, and have our being.

ABOUT THE AUTHOR

CLARE PRICE IS CEO of Octain Growth Systems, a global strategic planning consultancy that helps organizations grow to dominate their markets by accelerating business growth.

Clare developed the Octain Growth System (OGS) to enable organizations to replace time and money-wasting hit and miss marketing activities with a proven, turnkey marketing operating system that drives sustainable business success through improving marketing team performance and productivity.

Prior to launching Octain, Clare was a research director for Gartner's Internet Strategies Service. She also served as vice president of research for Demand Metric, a strategic marketing advisory service, where she led the research analysis team into cloud computing applications for marketing automation, social platforms, CPQ software, sales enablement, and cloud knowledge management.

Clare is the author of five marketing playbooks and the cyberthriller, *Web of Betrayal*. Her 2020 book, *Make Remote Work*, is a resource guide for achieving growth in the remote economy by effectively managing people, processes, and product development and distribution.

Clare has been a featured speaker for the American Marketing Association, Vistage, the California Society of Association Executives, Women in Technology International (WITI), eWomenNetwork, and the U.C. Davis Graduate School of Management.

Need help with implementing any of these steps or want to learn more about the OGS? Visit our website, www.octaingrowth.com where you can download our free resources, or set up a consultation with one of our Growth Architects.

Clare can be reached directly at clare@octaingrowth.com.

ENDNOTES

1. "The Cost of Hiring New Employees in Manufacturing," *Flexicrew* (blog), May 22, 2021, https://flexicrew.com/cost-of-hiring-new-employees-in-current-work-environment/.
2. Clare Price, *Make Remote Work* (Sacramento, CA: Octain Growth Systems, LLC, 2020).
3. Zapier Editorial Team, "Zapier Report: The 2021 State of Business Automation," *Zapier* (blog), April 20, 2021, https://zapier.com/blog/state-of-business-automation-2021/.
4. "PwC US Cloud Business Survey," *PwC*, May 12, 2021, https://www.pwc.com/us/en/tech-effect/cloud/cloud-business-survey.html.
5. Simon Sinek, *Find Your Why* (New York: Portfolio/Penguin, an imprint of Penguin Random House, LLC, 2017).
6. Axel Buether, Chair, Visual Communication, Wuppertal University, "Color Language — Effects of Color on Our Perception and Behaviour" (TEDx talk, December 11, 2017) "The Language of Color — Effects on Our Experience and Behavior", https://www.youtube.com/watch?v=oCNWPu0ScjA,
7. Clint Fontanella, "How to Calculate Customer Lifetime Value," *HubSpot* (blog), May 6, 2021, https://blog.hubspot.com/service/how-to-calculate-customer-lifetime-value.
8. Sophia Bernazzani, "The Ultimate Guide to Calculating, Understanding, and Improving CAC in 2021," *HubSpot* (blog), December 9, 2021, https://blog.hubspot.com/service/what-does-cac-stand-for.
9. www.octaingrowth.com
10. Jeffrey Gitomer and Randy Glasbergen, *Jeffrey Gitomer's Little Red Book of Selling: 12.5 Principles of Sales Greatness: How to Make Sales Forever* (Austin, TX: Bard Press, 2004).
11. Mark Curtis, Kevin Quiring, Bill Theofilou, and Agneta Björnsjö, "Life Reimagined, Mapping the Motivations that Matter for Today's Consumers" (Accenture Global Consumer Pulse Research, 2021).
12. "Which Types of B2B Influencer Content Do Buyers Find Valuable?" *Marketing Charts*, April 3, 2019.
13. Steve Harrison, Bradley Communications, *LinkedIn*, https://www.linkedin.com/company/bradley-communications/.
14. Sinek, *Find Your Why*.

15. W. Chan Kim and Renée Mauborgne, *Blue Ocean Strategy: How to Create Uncontested Market Space and Make the Competition Irrelevant* (Boston: Harvard Business Review Press, 2015).
16. Gerald Chait, "Half the Money I Spend on Advertising is Wasted; The Trouble is I Don't Know Which Half," *B2B Marketing* (blog), March 18, 2015.
17. Content Marketing Institute, "Enterprise Content Marketing," 2021.
18. Dennis Shiao, "Does Marketing Need to Generate a Profit?" *Content Corner*, November 12, 2021.
19. "What is Marketing Enablement," *Seismic*, https://seismic.com/enablement-explainers/what-is-marketing-enablement/.
20. *Gartner Glossary*, Gartner, Inc. 2022, https://www.gartner.com/en/glossary.
21. Ibid.
22. "What are Sales Enablement Platforms?" *Gartner Peer Insights*, Gartner, Inc., 2022, https://www.gartner.com/reviews/market/sales-enablement-platforms.
23. Whimsical, https://whimsical.com.
24. Miro, https://miro.com.
25. Product Marketing Alliance, https://www.productmarketingalliance.com/.
26. Product Marketing World, https://productmarketingworld.com/.
27. Sharebird. https://sharebird.com/.
28. Michael Mankins, "5 Ways the Best Companies Close the Strategy-Execution Gap," *Harvard Business Review*, November 20, 2017.
29. Aha!, https://www.aha.io.
30. Hootsuite, https://www.hootsuite.com.
31. monday.com, https://monday.com.
32. "The State and Fate of Small and Medium Businesses: SMBs and the Role of Innovation in Weathering the Pandemic," Xerox Corp., 2021.
33. Calendly, https://calendly.com.
34. TidyCal, https://tidycal.com.
35. TimeTap, https://www.timetap.com/index.html.
36. SimplyBook.me, https://simplybook.me/en/.
37. Legwork, https://www.legwork.com.
38. Mindbody, https://www.mindbodyonline.com/business.
39. Picktime, https://www.picktime.com/scheduling-software/hair-salon.
40. PandaDoc, https://www.pandadoc.com.
41. Proposify, https://www.proposify.com/.
42. Bidsketch, https://www.bidsketch.com.
43. Jami Oetting, "13 Proposal Software Tools for Proposal Creation and Management," *HubSpot* (blog), February 10, 2022, https://blog.hubspot.com/agency/proposal-software.

44. Gadjo Sevilla, "The Best Email Marketing Software for 2022," *PC Magazine*, December 9, 2021 https://www.pcmag.com/picks/the-best-email-marketing-software
45. Toma Kulbyte, "The Value of Customer Self-Service in the Digital Age," *SuperOffice* (blog), May 4, 2021.
46. Steven MacDonald, "9 Live Chat Software Benefits for 2021 (Backed by Data)," *SuperOffice* (blog), May 10, 2021, https://www.superoffice.com/blog/live-chat-software-benefits/.
47. Nancy Pekala, "How B2B Marketers are Leveraging Live Chat to Increase Sales," AMA Access, 2021
48. LiveChat, https://www.livechat.com.
49. Zendesk, https://www.zendesk.com.
50. Olark, https://www.olark.com.
51. US Bureau of Labor Statistics, "Job Openings and Labor Turnover — November 2021," news release no. USDL-22-0001, January 4, 2022, https://www.bls.gov/news.release/archives/jolts_01042022.pdf.
52. Ian Cook, "Who is Driving the Great Resignation?" *Harvard Business Review*, September 15, 2021.
53. Matt Schlegel, *Teamwork 9.0: Successful Workgroup Problem Solving Using the Enneagram*, (self-pub., 2020).
54. Ibid.
55. The Who-Do Method is a trademark of The People Catalysts, https://thepeoplecatalysts.com/.
56. Ibid.
57. Indeed Editorial Team, "What is Participative Leadership?" *Indeed* (blog), February 22, 2021, https://www.indeed.com/career-advice/career-development/participative-leadership.
58. Ken Blanchard and Phil Hodges, *The Servant Leader* (Thomas Nelson, March 11, 2003).
59. John C. Maxwell, *The 21 Irrefutable Laws of Leadership: Follow Them and People Will Follow You*, rev. ed. (HarperCollins Leadership, September 16, 2007).
60. Kimberly Layne, *Connections Change Everything* (Indie Books International, February 21, 2020).

CPSIA information can be obtained
at www.ICGtesting.com
Printed in the USA
JSHW021427271222
35405JS00006B/78